S0-BAT-424

YOU CAN BE

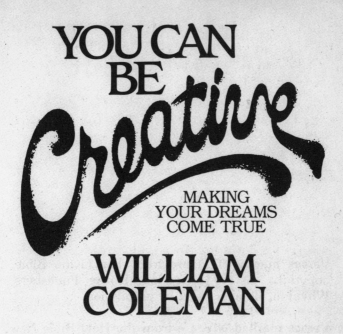

MAKING
YOUR DREAMS
COME TRUE

WILLIAM
COLEMAN

HARVEST HOUSE PUBLISHERS
Eugene, Oregon 97402

YOU CAN BE CREATIVE

Copyright © 1983 by Harvest House Publishers
Eugene, Oregon 97402

Library of Congress Catalog Card Number 83-080474
ISBN 0-89081-387-6

Printed in the United States of America.

Dedicated
to
Walter Hunt

His lasting genius helps hold us together.

The intelligent man is always open to new ideas.
In fact, he looks for them.

—Proverbs 18:15 TLB

CONTENTS

You Can Do It!

Every person is creative. The difference is that some people use their creative ability and others don't.

Creativity isn't restricted to painters, musicians, and pottery-makers. The good lawyer, housewife, mechanic, farmer, secretary, or teacher is also a creative person. Most of us need some guidance and encouragement to open our imaginations and let them move constructively.

God would never be content to lead a dull life. His creative mind stretches far beyond anything we have yet dreamed. When he decided to create a starfish, God didn't finish until He had made 2000 patterns! He created billions of people, and no two even smell exactly the same.

The Bible is filled with courage. Like a cheering section, it chants: "Go ahead—dream, investigate, experiment." Life is packed with undiscovered treasure. It's just waiting for Christians with open, daring minds to put them together.

Creativity enriches your personal life. It adds sparkle to the group you teach. And it can open a new world to the children under your roof.

—William L. Coleman
Aurora, Nebraska

Chapter One

What Are We Talking About?

You are a creative person. You have the potential to invent, innovate, and produce. From your mind can come imaginative and interesting ideas.

Let your mind travel back to childhood. Can you remember the brooms, sticks, and mops that you used for horses? Did you put together a local theater with a tattered array of costumes? Now the challenge is to awaken those sleeping instincts again.

For many people creativity fades as they grow older. They become well-hewn adults with most of their adventure chipped off. But there is hope for those who would like to reach out and create again. The channels which God has given can be opened again.

A creative person can be guided in this direction from childhood. But creativity can also be aroused for the first time in adults. The older we get, the harder it is to adapt to new practices, but it can be done.

Creativity does not mean to make something out of nothing. Only God can do that. Dr. David Dilling of Grace College has a simple definition of creativity: "Creativity is taking what is already existing and available and changing it in unpredictable ways. It is finding new and unique ways to solve problems."

Thomas Edison maintained a stable full of great minds just to create new ideas. They are responsible for many of the progressive innovations we now enjoy. From automobiles to electric knives, the story is one of pursuing dreams by many inventors.

Many people apparently believe that creativity is restricted to poets, painters, and composers. But in reality the art of creativity also belongs to housewives, mechanics, and farmers.

June is a 14-year-old who looks for creative ways to motivate herself. When she has a track meet scheduled, June writes notes to herself describing herself as a winner. These notes are tacked on her bulletin board and posted on her mirror. June has created ways to self-motivate.

Creativity becomes a useful tool in the hands of anyone who wants to use it. The person who needs to pack 16 pounds of meat into a 14-pound capacity freezer . . . the dad who needs to attend his son's ball game and a club meeting on the same night . . . the youth who wants to convince his parents that a "C" is a high grade for geometry—all of these people could apply some practical creativity.

Too many of us are sold out to the security of doing what we are told. Many of our lives have become highly regulated. We are told when to start work, exactly what procedure to follow, and when to go home. Performance is judged on our ability to *comply* rather than to *create*. New wrinkles are often stared at with suspicion.

Authorities have made the accusation that one of the major assassins of creativity has been our educational system. The teacher of a precollege high school class expressed his exasperation this way: "I hate to admit it, but most of our high academic achievers are the least creative students. Good grades often mean they have done what they were told. It also means they do not think for themselves."

Science News reports so much concern that educators are now considering "creativity" tests similar to I.Q. analyses. Some medical schools feel they have placed too much emphasis on high grades; they want to widen their search for capable problem-solvers.

In many cases creative students are rebellious. Often the creative student is restless because his thinking does not fit the mold. And yet his potential is enormous if it can be exercised correctly.

Dr. Dilling has been forced to conclude that formal education is presently a hindrance to creativity because the emphasis has been to *conform* rather than *explore*.

In defense of education, the dilemma should be explained. Teachers must give the basics of science, English, and history. Without these tools the creative mind has little to work with. The problem seems to be *the lack of compromise*. The tools must be provided with the latitude to explore. This difficulty presents swarms of problems for teachers, but it is the hurdle that must be overcome.

Education often courts extremes. For a period of time there is a tremendous emphasis on self-expression, with little regard given to facts. Then arises a cry for a return to the basics. The pendulum swings toward rote memory.

Dr. Joseph Bogan argues that too strict an emphasis on rational, logical, straight-line thinking is devastating. To encourage creativity, the student must be prompted to wander.

Even within the Christian world, where the unique and creative abilities of each person could be encouraged, there is a stifling influence in which originality is met with suspicion.

Often there is little room to exercise freedom of expression. Most people are judged by their ability to conform. Attempts to be different are greeted with suspicion.

Joe Bayly has written his concern: "A closed system, one in which all the answers are already in, is the enemy of creative thought and action.

Where the finality of Scripture is applied to every area of art and learning and life, creativity is killed."

A few years ago I tried an experiment with a group of junior high students. They were asked to divide into pairs and devise their own church service.

Some teams wanted the sermon at the beginning of the service. Others asked for more guitar music. Another picked out quicker hymns.

The extent of their creativity was to rearrange the service. No one suggested anything we had not done before. Their imaginations could not shake those boundaries. The average age was 13, and their thinking was cemented.

Compare that attitude with Ann's. She discovered some handcrafted dolls and decided to give one a try. She enjoyed making them so much that soon she was making them for friends. After prodding from her husband, Ann sold some to stores. Today Ann owns a successful business—because she dared stretch her creativity.

Creative thinking is what some authorities call adventurous thinking. This is the opposite of the closed-system variety, which is locked in by rules and regulations. For example, simple math is closed. Two apples plus three apples makes five apples.

Adventurous thinking is done when a class is asked to solve a problem by using all resources at its disposal. For example, how could a person make toys for needy children without spending money? Here is a chance to incorporate basic skills into a creative outlet.

Many of us will throw up our hands and say, "I'm not a creative person." Maybe you are deep in a trench of doing what you have seen and been told.

If a person is tacked down too tightly, he lacks the freedom to invent and improvise. If everything has to be just right, with no risks taken, fear prevents the person from creativity.

But don't despair—a person can acquire creativity. Try this simple exercise and you will see your creativity increase immediately. Take a piece of paper, a pencil, and a daily newspaper. Look at the newspaper and write down as many uses for it as you can. Do this for ten minutes.

Leave the materials and come back in 20 minutes. Now add five more uses. Your mind and skills are beginning to expand. You are starting to climb out of a rut.

Try another exercise which may be of more direct benefit. Sit down and make a list of all the ways you could save energy and money in your house. If you like, brainstorm with the rest of the family. It will increase their creativity.

Some authorities tell us we could cut back on energy use by 25 percent without seriously changing our lifestyle. Doesn't it feel satisfying to create with a purpose?

The person who creates is not usually the one without restrictions. To have no restrictions at all leads to aimlessness. The more likely candidate is the person with *limited freedom*. His boundaries are narrow enough to give him security yet they are wide enough to offer him liberty. There is enough rope to roam but not enough to get lost.

The same rules apply to groups and families. If a meeting has an open spirit, it can result in creative proposals. If it is without rules, it ends in anarchy.

A family discussion mixed with respect and freedom has the potential of ingenious input. The dinner table where dad rules as a total despot offers little hope.

Because creativity is the arranging of existing things, all of us can be creative. We all have access to things and situations that we can change. It can be done by merely calling on the resources we already have.

An excellent college student had proved himself both academically and athletically. But he still had a dream: He wanted to do woodwork.

Finally he decided to do something about his dreams. He picked up an old piece of furniture at a sale and painstakingly turned it into a television cabinet. Friends remarked on its beauty and said, "I didn't know you had it in you."

He had it in him but he had never tried drawing it together before. Granted, it is a fairy tale to dream we can do everything. But most of us can create in far more areas than we are presently aware.

Creative people are looking for change. Those who are happy with everything the way it is can never create.

One 37-year-old man felt he had always been trapped in a routine life. His insides called out to do something different. He tried out for the local community play. To his surprise he landed a leading role, and the play was a smashing success.

Afterward people wanted to know if he had been in high school plays or in college productions. But the only plays he had performed in were the ones in his heart. He needed to become fed up with boredom.

A study group at Berkeley made a report on creative people. They were found to be adventurers who had taken giant steps toward becoming the persons they were capable of being.

Intelligence seems to play a role in creativity, but it is by no means crucial. More important are the spirit of adventure and a good sense of humor.

The adventurer cannot guarantee the outcome. He is willing to take a chance.

Humor is necessary because we dare not take ourselves too seriously. If I do not leave open the option to laugh at myself, I am too uptight. A slightly slanted outlook is at the core of creativity.

Tests have demonstrated that creative people have a healthy intelligence. However, I.Q. is not the deciding factor.

I talked to a college student with great mental prowess. We discussed creativity in relationship to his future plans. His hope was to become a lawyer, and he saw no room for creativity in the field.

I hope he will soon be introduced to the wide scale of creative law practice. Hopefully he will see how lawyers have used exact science to change the world.

If a group of people are open to change, they may be able to brainstorm in collective creativity. Mutual trust is an essential ingredient.

Make a list of new things you would like to see in your home, on the job, and in your personal life. Imagine that money and personalities are of no consequence. Do this for ten minutes. Take a 20-minute break. Come back and add five more ideas.

You are stretching your mind, and your creativity is growing.

Dr. Dilling sums it up this way: "There seems to be plenty of evidence that everyone has the potential for creative thought; however, we differ in the talents we have for expressing these. Probably the most important thing we can do to increase our output of creative thoughts is to learn to relax and let our mind go free."

Probably most people are all for change. But many people seem to want creative change only as long as it isn't different—a strange contradiction in terms!

This discussion has given us a rough survey of what makes a creative person. There are exceptions, and this must be remembered. Nevertheless, the basic ingredients are the same. Here is a brief resume' of creative qualities:

1. Fair amount of intelligence

2. Thirst for adventure
3. Sense of humor
4. Feeling of restlessness

Knowledge helps, but it sometimes leads to blind acceptance. Artistic skill is impressive, but it may be restricted to the aesthetic.

In its broadest outline the four qualities we noted are the most significant. The person with these fundamental traits can be taught to heighten his creativity.

When Thomas Edison assembled some of America's best minds in a laboratory, his sole purpose was to stretch their minds and take years to invent and discover. The most important question in the lab was, "Gentlemen, are you having a good time?" Those who enjoyed creating were clever enough to explore. They were surprised with joy.

A major role played by God in the universe is as Creator. It has been a part of His life historically, and it continues in men's lives today. Made in His image and personality, we are invited to play a part in His ongoing creativity.

Exercise

1. Who is the most creative person you know? Describe the person.
2. Name one problem in your home. List four ways to solve it.

3. Would you consider your friends to be creative? Explain.
4. Write down ten uses for a brick. You can do anything with the brick except build.

Chapter Two

Fear of Creativity

The whole world is stacked against the creative person. Ever since he was a small child the story has been the same: He wins approval, recognition, and even love by *conforming*. Distrust, coolness, and hostility are the rewards of those who refuse to fit the pattern.

But some will object: What about Edison, Picasso, and Wesley? They were acclaimed because of their ability to be different. The world has piled money and fame at their feet. That's true. However, two things chase us back to reality. These names are the rare exceptions and not the norm. They also accomplished their feats through enormous pain.

The tide didn't sweep them to the shores of success. They fought, kicked, and crawled for every inch, especially in their early days.

Creativity is not idle dallying. In most cases it emerges after hard work and awesome resistance. Sometimes the greatest friction comes from inside oneself. We try desperately to muster up enough courage to do differently. Our imagination struggles, leaps forward, then backs off to regroup. After hours, maybe days, of fencing, our creative idea backs down exhausted. It fought vigorously and lost without ever leaving the shell of our mind.

It is painful to create. It hurts to have a child. Butterflies struggle out of cocoons. Light comes from heat. Strength builds on friction. There are exceptions, but basically these are the rules of life.

Admitting this fact, many people will drop out before they start. They enjoy the pedestrian ventures of life. The dependable, the routine, even the monotonous have appeal for them. Their creativity will probably remain restricted to small, simple pursuits—maybe some doodling on paper or a story to amuse the children. They will always be creative people, but they have decided to keep their creativity contained. That's where most of us live.

Jesus told a story which deals directly with our problem. He talked about a man who distributed talents to his servants. The gentleman was going on a trip and wanted them to invest the money while he was gone.

When the master returned, he discovered that the first two had invested well. However, the third servant had dug a hole in the ground and buried his coin. He decided to play it safe. The risk of investing was too great to take.

The servant explained, "So I was afraid and went out and hid your talent in the ground" (Matthew 25:25 NIV). His master was furious. He poured out threats and punishment on the timid tightwad.

Why did Christ tell the story? Was it an attempt to prod loose the fearful? He was concerned about people who were burying what God had given them—those who were afraid to try something daring.

Creativity is the happy expectation of life. There are exciting things to do, great arrays of combinations to try, countless avenues to travel. We need to see new adventures as beneficial and worth the risk. A bird simply doesn't soar well with his wings close to his chest.

Maybe we spend too much time erecting borders. Our parents were naturally concerned about our safety. They told us the stove was hot, stairs were dangerous, and wall sockets can shock people. In some atmospheres there was little of "try this, see if it works."

We tried an experiment with our three children. The idea came from a show that my wife and I had watched. The children were given the option to participate or not. They all elected to do it.

Each child (ages 13, 11, and 9) was given his share of the food budget for one week. They could spend the money on anything they wanted. If they bought a week's supply of candy the first day, they received no criticism. The choices were entirely theirs.

However, if they ran out of money they would get no food from us. They would have to dip into their savings to complete the seven days. If they had money left over, it was theirs to keep.

We gave them nothing. A slice of butter from our larder cost them a penny, as did salt and sugar. One day Mary bought a dish of ice cream for ten cents.

When the children shopped, some interesting patterns developed. None of them purchased their favorite breakfast cereal. They quickly discovered how expensive it was. All of them bought the school lunches. Some rapid math proved they couldn't pack a lunch for 50 cents. They didn't buy candy because they couldn't afford it. None of them ate out because the budget wouldn't stand it.

The first week each one lost a little money, but immediately they wanted to try again. The second week they saved about two dollars apiece!

They are anxious to do it again, and we will. Each had a feeling of independence, responsibility, and creativity. They could express their own tastes, expand their imaginations, and learn the value of a dollar.

Most adults feel more secure when they can keep the lid on. Parents, teachers, and counselors are often afraid of granting much freedom. After all, "there is no telling what children will do when left to themselves." But this is often a reflection of the adult's need for security. He has to be in complete control or else he might not be able to handle the situation.

When life is put in this context, creativity takes the form of rebellion. The person who strides out to do something new feels like Sandra Day O'Connor going to the Supreme Court. It is a first-class emotional upheaval. Creativity attacks and drains the individual in almost leech fashion. It sucks, weakens, and frightens because of the system in which he must operate.

The author of Proverbs paints the attitude of many people toward creativity: "The slothful man saith, . . . a lion is in the streets" (26:13 KJV). He pulls the cover over his head and goes back to sleep.

An innovative person agrees with the slothful—there might be a beast stalking the sidewalks. But he wants to go out and see it. How tall are lions? Do they really have flowing manes? Can they be bridled and ridden? What kind of pet does a lion make?

All sorts of risks are possible. The key difference is *attitude*. For some people a lake is a place to swim, fish, and sail. For others it is a dangerous body of water to be avoided. The people have equal ability and the lake doesn't change its dimension; the attitude rests on the question of *what someone wants to make of it*.

As we have mentioned, creativity is an extremely practical matter. The person who wants to redecorate his home is tinkering with genius. He sees combinations which he genuinely admires. Another person's home looks both striking and comfortable. But after tempting the genies of diversity, he retreats to a quiet, conventional motif.

He struggles inside with the things he really likes. Then he capitulates to the least controversial approach. He almost soared with the eagles, but he finally decided to remain with the penguins.

The person who did decorate his living room in a highly personal style took a risk. People may laugh at him. He may later become displeased with the results. But he is determined to take a leap.

One Midwestern dreamer decided to drop out of college and dare a little. He wanted to try his wings in the world of commerce.

Looking around for something different, his eyes rested on a cow chip lying in a field. On the woodless plains our ancestors used these mini-mounds constructively. Buffalo chips were used as fuel and sometimes helped patch sod houses. Now cow chips dot the countryside serving as fertilizer and traps for careless boots.

A light went on in this young man's vigorous imagination. He treated and baked a chip mound. A pen and holder were then stuck on top. They are called "Bull Pens" and sell presently for 12 dollars. He has manufactured thousands of these, and his creative mind is looking for a new project.

Somewhere in the process he decided how to handle criticism. What would relatives, neighbors, and former teachers say? Surely he is demented and debased. What kind of warped cranium would conjure this up?

He fought the fear of creativity. The result was a funny, imaginative, and lucrative product.

The challenge of creativity pivots on a fundamental choice. Which do we prize more—security or freedom? The majority of people will vote for security every time.

There was a time when we were terribly concerned over daydreaming—a terrific fear of what we considered "idle" minds. Now we are learning to appreciate a healthy amount of mental adventurism.

Mark Twain was an excellent daydreamer. His mind could travel the rivers and search for animals along the shore. The talented author never finished grade school, but Americans have enjoyed his fertile imagination for a century. Samuel Langhorne Clemens even "dreamed up" his new name.

Einstein used to daydream about the universe. What would happen if man could fly through space at the speed of light?

Not all of life can become a daydream. Someone has to lay the concrete streets and cook dinner. But some stargazing and mind-stretching should be encouraged.

Paul wrote a passage which should serve as a challenge to all Christians: "Do not conform any longer to the pattern of this world, but

be transformed by the renewing of your mind"
(Romans 12:2 NIV).

Ask yourself frankly: Do you see this verse as
a red light or a green one? Those of us who see
it only as a prohibition are saying some serious
things about ourselves. We may imagine God as
a restricting warden. But others will see Him as
a friend freeing us.

The verse says that we are bogged down and
shackled to the evil patterns of this world. We
are often stuck in a wasteful, dull, unimaginative
way of life. God wants to do some things with
our minds which we have never done before. He
will renew, rebuild, recharge our brains. God will
help us create.

But some will retort that it sounds risky. There
is no telling where this type of approach might
lead. *That is exactly the point.* Those who are
afraid of it will stay close to the vest. The excep-
tion will push fear behind and fly to new worlds
and new patterns.

Opportunity and danger are often inseparable.
Sometimes the scent of danger should wake us
up. The risk involved may give us the hint of
something worthwhile. If there is a price to pay,
our venture may be valuable.

Rollo May reminds us of the restrictions of
daydreaming *(The Courage to Create)*. Perpetual
dreamers are of little benefit. They spend their
entire lives pondering the possibilities. Many of
us fall into this category. We are forever making plans in our minds, but we get nothing done.
We are endless dreamers.

One night I listened to an interesting guest on a television talk show. After a lackluster selling career he opened a lost-dog agency. Some people offer large rewards for the recovery of lost pets. The pets have been like members of the family, and their owners will pay hundreds or even thousands of dollars for their return.

This gentleman went to work on the idea, and now he has a prosperous business. When I heard his business approach I reacted immediately, "Hey, that was my idea!" And it was true. I had thought of doing it and had mentioned it to my wife. But there was a drastic difference between this man and me: I had *the idea,* but he had *the idea and the business.*

More than one person who reads this chapter can identify with the problem. He has an idea incubating in his mind for years. So far he has been afraid to give birth to it. If he does not allow it to see the break of day, the idea may eventually die from lack of exposure.

Every avenue of life calls for creativity. Rather than swim in the high waters of indecision, try this approach. Take a pencil and paper and isolate an idea. Write down one thing you have often wanted to do—something you consider imaginative, helpful, even fun.

Now list five things you can do about your idea. These are action steps, essential to carrying out creativity. The first point may be to talk to someone. The second could be to check the library for information. Number three might be to write a letter to investigate further. Number four is to possibly make a drawing. Number five could be to accumulate materials.

Each project calls for a different five steps. But now you are off to a start. A birth is beginning. It will hurt to take action, but what a pleasure as you watch it come to life!

As soon as one step is completed, begin to make plans for the second. Will it take a phone call, a trip, a pencil?

Moses was once faced with a frustrating situation. He was exhausting his energy. Everything he did seemed to put him further behind. The famous leader was trying to rule probably 250,000 people by himself.

God moved into Moses' life and gave him some constructive ideas to carry out. He sent the instructions by way of Jethro, Moses' father-in-law.

Jethro said, "This is your problem: You are wearing yourself out. Here is your solution: Organize step-by-step. Appoint judges over the people—someone to rule the thousands, then someone for the hundreds, the fifties, and the tens." Each step was aimed at putting a creative idea to work. When all of them were completed, the young nation was revolutionized. Moses lived to be a ripe old age, and justice was distributed to Israel (Exodus 18).

Many of us come from an ultracautious background. The first questions we learn to ask are often negative. Why won't this idea work? It is expensive, time-consuming, too unconventional—and the list circles the globe. This becomes a fixed mental attitude. The minute a new proposal rears its head in our mind, we bombard it with pessimism. We may become the world's leading authority on what won't work.

In some ways a mind can be trained in the same way as a hand or foot. We can learn to throw a ball or ice skate. We can also begin to think positively after years of negative reactions.

Dr. Liam Hudson tells us we spend a lot of our efforts repressing creativity. When we are awake, new ideas are frequently trying to dive into our thinking process. We flick them off like mosquitoes. Our mind starts to daydream, and when we catch ourselves we snap back to reality. We are concerned with more productive pursuits. Dr. Hudson's studies indicate that we may even resist dreams at night. The person who is afraid to create seems to shake off ideas even in his sleep.

It is similar to having company call on a Saturday afternoon. Some people can put everything down and make a guest feel like a rich uncle. Others will turn the visitor off immediately and be impatient.

We handle creative ideas the same way. Whether they remain or slip away depends on their reception.

The changing of attitude often comes by practice. When a new idea invades the perimeter of our mind we say, "Let's give it a try." We then travel down a positive road as far as we can. If nothing stops a good idea, we go with it until the happy completion.

Imagine an excellent athlete arriving at a

renowned track meet. Before the events begin, a television announcer presses an interview.

"Biff, tell our audience what you hope to accomplish today."

"Sure thing. I hope to keep the old records. I'm proud of what Jesse Owens and Bob Matthias did. I've got to be careful not to break those."

Our fear of change makes about as much sense!

The ability to relax is at the heart of creativity. It's difficult to be at ease when we're afraid.

There is a vast difference between fear and appreciation. At times we want to preserve the old because it is the best. We need never apologize for this. But it is quite another matter to become frozen out of fear, to say that we will not change because we are afraid of what might happen.

"For God did not give us a spirit of timidity, but a spirit of power, of love and of self-discipline" (2 Timothy 1:7 NIV).

Some reluctance to fail is healthy. But extreme anxiety over failure leaves many of us noncreative.

All of us get wild ideas once in a while. How about a dinner plate that doesn't need to be washed (simply eat it as part of the meal, like a taco shell)? Possibly a lightweight porta-copter (people could fly just a few feet off the ground and maneuver around town)?

They are no more or less silly than airplanes, Frisbees, or polio vaccine. Each idea seems so distant, and yet it may be only as far away as our courage.

How absurd can a Pet Rock be? But someone sold many thousands of them. Can any idea be simpler than painted clothespins? Yet they sell in shops all across the country.

Joe Davis saw the utility workers changing the old bronze lights in Whitefish Bay, Wisconsin. He made a quick call to the electric company and took a risk. He paid 5 dollars each for 63 street lights. The risk was a loss of 315 dollars and some ridicule from his friends.

But instead of being humiliated, he successfully sold them for 35 dollars each. His chance turned over 2205 dollars in commerce!

Recently a Sherman Oaks, California, corporation decided to print and sell a "nothing" credit card. It is good for nothing. The carrier cannot charge anything on it. The card is a phony.

The front sports a picture of Millard Fillmore. Their motto is "Go now, pay now." It is completely, thoroughly, and absolutely useless.

This prize package, including instructions, sells for $2.85. So far 150,000 cards have been sold. That is close to half a million dollars in commerce!

But maybe your mind doesn't run this way. You are not looking for gimmicks or novelties. The problems you encounter at home, job, and church are real. Remember, the principles are the same no matter how serious the goal. Those who are afraid of failing will not create. Anyone whose aim in life is to avoid pain will not create. The path of least resistance is to go with what presently exists. Put a pillow in your rut and make it into a bed. Soon it becomes comfortable.

Whoever thought of putting bookracks in grocery stores and other businesses created a boom. Today millions of individuals are reading Christian literature in unprecedented amounts. Highway travelers stop in restaurants and leave with a book they never expected to read. Someone had an idea, and he decided to do something about it. He was prepared to fail if necessary.

Exercise

1. Make a list of four ideas. Don't stop until you have four.
2. Pick one idea from the list. Give five reasons why it is a good idea.
3. List five initial steps you can take to get your idea started.
4. Share the creative idea with a group or person. Get some healthy input.
5. Start taking the steps to implement the idea.
6. Solve this problem: A father and son were attending a ball game when the stands collapsed. The boy was critically injured and rushed to the hospital. The surgeon looked at the lad and exclaimed, "I can't operate on this boy; he is my son." How could this happen?

The surgeon was his mother.

Chapter Three

Mind Expansion

Your creative skills can be increased tremendously. A few simple steps will help stretch your mind to possibilities it has never known.

A staff at the University of Georgia believes this so thoroughly that it had developed a Studies of Creative Behavior Department. One goal is to increase creative thinking.

A few years ago the director, Paul Torrance, began the National Future Problem Solving Bowl. Annually over 200 students from grades 4-12 enter the contest. Contestants are given specific problems to solve in a creative fashion. They deal with ambitious projects such as underwater colonization or space challenges.

National awards are given for original thought and practical solutions. Each age group has it own winners.

As with most skills, creativity needs to be learned and exercised. The following are some suggestions to expand our mind and make it more fertile for new and exciting ideas. This is only a starter list. Add your own creative ideas.

Increase your knowledge in a wide area. Often we are starved for ideas because we are not learning. Give yourself a quick test. What do you know that you did not know seven days ago? Be specific. What have you learned about gardening, hula dancers, Chinese food, compost piles, and computers?

If you have collected little or no new knowledge during the past week, you are a dry well. It is impossible to pump something out.

Knowledge doesn't come only from thick books or eternal lectures. Magazines, some television shows, newspapers, and conversations have bits of information that you can pick up and store.

Henry Luce, former publisher of *Time* magazine, had a rich habit. When he met someone, Luce peppered him with questions. Where had he been? What had he seen? What did he think? What had he tried?

While Luce was talking he was not learning. While he was asking questions his world was stretching and his mind expanding.

Andrew Carnegie literally had more money than he knew what to do with. He searched for a way to be the greatest and best influence with it. Finally he set the goal of dotting America with free libraries. Carnegie paid for 10,000 libraries because he thought the best way to help a community was to give it the resources to help itself. There is no way to calculate how many creative ideas these institutions have fostered. Libraries are excellent places to browse and collect new perspectives. There are id as on those shelves that you would never have imagined.

You don't have to be an authority to create, but you do need to know something about the subject.

Suppose you want to begin a woodworking hobby. Trial-and-error can be a painful and expensive route. A little knowledge can put you in the position of creating.

Someone says, "I want to be a creative thinker. Don't tell me anything." His job is almost impossible.

Learn to appreciate daydreaming. Daydreaming, more than an idle escape, is often the embryo of exciting experiences.

Most of us daydream. Some of us sit in offices and picture ourselves driving golf balls across plush fairways. Others of us peel potatoes in kitchens while fantasizing about skating over frozen ponds. Is this a frivolous waste of time? No! It's a way to discover ourselves and our potential.

Daydream while you are reading this book.

Jot down some of the thoughts you have.

What are two changes you would like to see in your club? Be specific. How would you go about explaining these changes to the other members? What benefits would they have? Practice describing them.

That exercise allowed you to put some thoughts together. You have created a rough pattern, and now you can transport these creative ideas to the real scene. Your daydream can become parent to the fact.

The person who has trouble dreaming will also have trouble acting.

Maybe you used to dream, but your life has met with repeated failures. It will be harder to dream again, but you can do it. Daydreaming can be the beginning of your new life. Be courageous. Picture yourself on top, winning, accomplishing, satisfied. The ability to dream is the foundation of a full and challenging life.

When my girl's bike tire loses air, we need to get it to the service station quickly. We can roll it while there is still some air left. If it goes completely flat the whole job will be harder.

Pump up those dreams while there are still some of them left. Learn to love constructive dreaming.

Prize curiosity. The lack of curiosity murders creativity. All of us have a certain amount of curiosity. I wonder how magicians make women disappear. It is a complete mystery to me how they can drive swords through people.

These are fruitless curiosities because I have never tried to discover the answers.

Those who rise up to a searching curiosity are the people who stretch and pull. A child's creative mind wants to know if something bounces. The curious mind asks, "What would happen if. . .?" The noncreative mind thinks it already knows—or worse yet, it doesn't care.

Albert Einstein knew Newton's laws and understood them. This was true of other people too. Fortunately, he had the vital ingredient of a curious, creative mind and asked, "What would happen if. . .?" When we assume we already know what will happen, creative curiosity dies.

Children have a great amount of curiosity. If we have lost our curiosity, don't blame it on maturity or adulthood. We have lost more than our youth; we have forfeited our right to create.

Feed curiosity. Starve it to death and creativity dies.

Seek opposite viewpoints. It is hard to listen to the other side, especially after we have made up our minds. Once you have selected a political party it is boring and painful to listen to someone from the opposite camp.

If I surround myself with those who agree with me, I will not grow. We reinforce what we already believe. We build on what exists and never break new ground.

A creative mind has to cherish new, different, even opposing materials. By its very nature, creative thought has to go against the grain.

I had a book which disagreed with my professor's position. When I showed it to him his reaction was adamant. "Throw it away!" was his response. Why was it a threat to him? With that type of endorsement of course I kept it, read it, and still have it.

I have a minister friend who does not come from my direction at all. He believes some of the oddest doctrines. However, almost every time I talk with him I see something about Jesus Christ I had not seen before.

Listen to your teenager's point of view. Hear an idea or argument that you don't appreciate. The potential for creative growth is enormous!

Are you capable of changing your mind? When was the last time you did? When did someone convince you to take another position? A person does not expand his mind by merely rehearsing what he already believes.

A teacher in Missouri held a trial in her high school class. She decided to try President Truman for his decision to drop the atom bomb. It was no easy task, since each student had to do extensive research.

The students visited the Truman Library. Pretend witnesses were called before a selected jury. Lawyers were appointed to each side.

Cries went up from the public that this was unfair and nonproductive. Others defended the creative teaching aid as highly motivational.

The teacher couldn't guarantee what the verdict would be. This was up to the students. Creativity was promoted in an open atmosphere in which both sides could be presented.

Two famous comedians were recently depicted on television. Their biographer said they started to lose popularity when they refused to change. They liked the old routines and felt safe and secure using them. When others recommended something new they brushed it aside.

The person who thinks he has all the truth nailed down cannot create. He believes that everything has already been created. Those who say, "I don't want to hear both sides; it's too confusing," will not create because it is too perplexing.

Open your imagination. The first cousin to daydreaming is *imagination*. If we prize imagination as productive and healthy, we can stretch our experience and our potential.

Public speaking falls into this category. The person who imagines himself taking charge of an audience is likely to do so. He sees himself telling fascinating stories or holding a captivating visual. Because his vision centers on success, his odds multiply greatly. If before you speak you can see yourself floundering and stammering, it often becomes a self-fulfilling prophecy.

I cannot imagine myself living on a South Sea island. I don't know the language. Fried bananas and coconut punch give me pimples. Because my imagination has flunked the South Sea island vision, my body has flunked it without ever getting there.

Imagine yourself in a Mongolian restaurant.

What is your reaction? Will you take the safest route and order American food? Will you stretch your imagination and order a new and exciting dish? Today you could enjoy something you have never known before.

We have a number of homemade family games. Some are so outrageous that my children would be embarrassed if I told you how we played them. But to see they are just plain fun. There is a time to buy a game, and there is also a time to take out our imagination and create our own game.

Imagination plays a vital role in goal-setting. What would you like to be doing ten years from now? If you can see yourself as a manager or president, your odds of reaching it are increased dramatically. If you imagine yourself sponsoring a refugee family this year, you can probably do it.

Love the word "why." Parents hate the word. Children are always peppering them with it. Why do children take piano lessons? Why do some teachers prohibit calculators in school?

Maybe we have learned to treat "why" as an unwelcome intruder when it can be the springboard to a beautiful future.

Do yourself a favor: List five important "whys." What are some questions you would like to ask?

"Why?" is like putting an idea in an incubator. It is preparing a new life to be born. Whys can give hope where only dullness existed before.

Isaac Watts was a teenager who asked why. He couldn't understand why the congregation sang in the same monotonous manner every Sunday. When he received no satisfactory answer he began to write new music and soon it was being sung all over Christendom. It started with a why.

Can you imagine the first person to throw a football? Previously it was a running and kicking game. Someone asked, "Why don't they throw it? If you make it spiral, it travels though the air like a bullet."

Sometime when you are reading the New Testament note all the times people asked why. Jesus continuously asked His audience why. They in turn asked why right back. It was a fertile ground for learning, investigation, and discovery.

Read inspirational stories. People with less skills than you have are doing amazingly creative things. Their stories and examples can be a tremendous inspiration.

Some of us are armchair creators. We read a story, think about it, and appreciate it, but we never *do* anything except read another story! Yet some of us are mysteriously moved. Be one of those.

How can a person with one leg ski? How can a blind person play the piano? How can a team play basketball without leaving their wheelchairs? There is so much more than ability involved. Consider their courage and creativity.

Search the Scriptures. The Bible is a

powerful book of creative action and thoughts. It will stretch your mind.

Christ will cause us to become creative thinkers as we have never been before. He saw life differently than we do. He saw God from a different perspective. He saw love, prejudice, and objects in a new light.

Our biggest hindrance is our insistence on reading our thinking into the Scriptures. The more we begin to see life from Christ's view, the broader our creative living will become. Creative thinking and activity are a by-product of His direct influence.

Someone in our community has built and is manufacturing a fascinating invention—a maternity chair. Instead of lying down to give birth, the mother is in a sitting position.

People of knowledge aren't afraid to expand their minds!

Exercise

1. Write an ad for crabgrass seed. Why should I plant it?
2. Make an exciting title for a short story about a diamond theft.
3. List six sources where you can get new ideas.
4. Design a Band-Aid dispenser.
5. Draw six lines and place a letter at the beginning

of each line. Write a six word sentence in which the words begin with these letters (and, or, in, an, etc. can be added).

T _____ E _____ S _____

B _____ H _____ N _____ .

Chapter Four

Father of Creativity

"God would never lead a boring life."

Weigh that sentence in your mind. How you react to it may greatly determine how creative you are going to be. If you picture God as resting, complacent, and living in the past, you have little hope. Those who see Him as alert, imaginative, and involved in creation have a spectacular future.

We are all affected by our theology. Muslim thinking is affected by Muslim theology. Japanese thinking is affected by Shintoism. Dedicated Christians are swayed to a high degree by how they see God.

Early missionaries taught the Cherokee Indians that playing and frivolity were evil. They saw God as representing stern, relentless justice. With Him everything was serious business. If we see God this way, it is difficult to feel fun and humor.

This is why the question cannot be ignored: Do you see God as creative and imaginative? If your answer is no, break your pencils and throw away your doodles.

Darkness and a fear of God often go hand-in-hand. It is hard to feel creative if we feel that creativity will anger God. To accept God as liberating and open to new ideas is to welcome change and progress.

Thinkers who tried to break out of this pattern met with tremendous hostility. New views of the universe, science, and medicine were held as pagan. Most doctors believed that the Black Plague was started by a strange position of the planets. Even the prestigious University of Paris was affected by this fossilization.

Look at the character of our Father: God has been fully enveloped in the act of creation; God continues to be part of the creative process; God will be part of the creative genius of the future.

In initial creation, God caused people, plants, gorillas, and fleas to live and breathe. This is only the tip.

The creation of a starfish is no small feat. But did you know that God created 2000 varieties?

I had heard coyotes howl in Kansas. Then I learned that God made 19 different types of coyote, and this doesn't count the wolf and dog relatives!

On a picnic you will probably meet ants. Did you know that there are army ants which build bridges over each other and bivouac in trees? Carpenter ants which live in wood? Tailor ants which sew homes from leaves? Slave ants which are raised to feed their master red ants? Ants which milk aphids for honeydew? Why didn't God just create an ant? Why so much variety and personality? Do you get the feeling He might have enjoyed it?

Check out the night sky. I won't try to guess how many stars there are, but there are billions of billions. Space is so vast that if you could travel at the speed of light (186,000 miles per second) it would take you four years to get to the first star outside the sun!

What about the size of these stars? The earth would fit into the sun a million times, yet the sun is only a medium-sized star; some stars are a thousand times larger than the sun!

God is the biggest supporter of creative life. He may be constantly hoping we will let our minds stretch...to build a better world...to extend life expectancy...to find a better energy source...to find a cure...to feed the world.

We ask, "Why doesn't God do something?" He may be asking, "Why don't *you* do something?"

God is dedicated to change! Malachi 3:6 says, "I am the Lord—I do not change" (TLB). God does not change His character, but He continuously changes His practices. There are things He did 2000 years ago which He has given up. He is in no rut. No one will find Him in the clutches of boredom. "So we can plainly see that God's method changed, for Christ, the new High Priest. . .came with the rank of Melchizedek" (Hebrews 7:15 TLB)

One of God's favorite words seems to be "new." The Bible mentions new creatures, new names, new heavens, new earths, new Jerusalem, a new song, a new commandment, new covenant, newness of life, and even being new every morning. God isn't dedicated to yesterday!

God has two basic methods of creating: He can create out of nothing, as He did when the universe and earth originated, or He can create out of existing materials, today and in the world to come.

God puts three essential ingredients together: 1) idea or intellect, 2) will to bring into existence, 3) carry-through.

Many of us have the first two qualities but we flunk when it comes to completion. God excelled in all three and even produced beautiful angels (Colossians 1:16).

God is not a mere witness of creativity; He is no grandstand spectator but creativity's precise father. He is its promoter and champion, its prime example.

The call goes out that it's all right to be different, imaginative, and creative. There is no eternal mandate to repeat the past.

What would God do if He were human? Would

He use His imagination to broaden the world He lived in, or would He fade into the scenery and go unnoticed?

I will not try to answer for God. The closest we can come is to look at the life of Jesus Christ. How did He conduct himself? What was His attitude toward creative change?

Christ led no crusade to call for a return to the good old days. He wasn't pouting, "If we were only back in the desert with Moses, things would be a lot better." Rather, His audiences were startled at the daringly different things He said and did. They spent half the time with their lower jaws dropped.

Sometime trace the word *marvel* through the New Testament and pick up the tenor. Christ's associates were not comforted by His staid, conventional approach. They were exhilarated by His refreshing approach.

I have a friend who is a fascinating speaker; what he says borders on the outrageous. What kind of speaker was Christ? One fact we can count on: He was anything but dull. People walked away talking to themselves. They were either excited or angry, but they were never bored. Christ was too new and interesting for that. People marveled at His answers.

They were also struck by His novel behavior. His disciples found Him talking alone with a Samaritan woman. They held their tongues but they couldn't believe their eyes (John 4:27 NIV). He was doing what men were not supposed to do.

After Christ gave His practical Sermon on the

Mount, Matthew tells us, "The crowds were amazed at his teaching" (7:28 NIV). It was undeniably different from what they had been hearing.

Jesus was not persecuted or executed because He was copying what everyone else was saying; He was not hated because he blended in. No man spoke or acted as this man—break out the ropes, hoist the cross. How can we trust anyone this different? Christ refused to merely trace the mistakes of the past. He was a novelty.

It then becomes ironic to see ourselves become pea-pod Christians. Blandness is an insult to Christ's creativity. Parroting what others say is a drab defeat for the life of a child of God.

God never said that creativity has come to an end. We are created in His image and with some of His potential. When you and I build on His creativity, we are following His example.

Are you trying to create a new method of literature distribution? How about a creative toy to make your child's heart happy? Or a way to make family togetherness more fun? Can you hear God cheering you on? The father of creativity is also its greatest promoter.

Exercise

1. Name three things Jesus did which were different.

2. Other than mankind, name two things you consider amazing creations by God.
3. Imagine that a person's mouth were not where it is. Where else could you put it?
4. Draw 12 round heads. Add ears, nose, mouth, hair, etc. without making any two alike.
5. What changes can you imagine God might like to see you make in your thinking?

Chapter Five

Mother of Creativity

If God is the father of creativity, then need is its mother—the need to do something. Need could be a demanding problem which shouts for a solution. It might be an improvement like a better ink pen. Need can also be a desire to accomplish, paint, mold, or be the best stilt-walker in your neighborhood.

Though not every need is vital, each is the call to create.

Some of the most creative ideas are born out of sheer boredom. Your uncle had nothing to do. He started working in his garage. Before long he created Alfred, the man made out of spare bolts, springs, and a fender. Children love Alfred. He has no real purpose except to make people smile.

Creativity makes a poor roach. A roach hides neatly in the woodwork or under a rug. Creativity is the opposite of skirting or avoiding problems. It is the determination to walk out, face the need, grab it by both horns, and start to wrestle it to the ground.

A person says, "I enjoy doing nothing." Carve a headstone for his creativity.

Another person is a directionless dreamer. His imagination is wild and fertile. He can picture the basement wall with beautiful butterscotch paint. He can see a flourishing business downtown. In his dreams he sees himself addressing the city council and dramatically changing minds.

He is a carryout soft drink—lots of ice but not much soda.

Creativity takes time to dream about a problem, but then it gets up and tries to solve it. Creativity does not study and catalog needs, but takes steps toward solving them.

Listen to ourselves in a gripe session: We enumerate all the problems—but it is the creative person who gets up and begins to solve them.

Practical creativity is *problem-solving*. Sometimes it solves problems as they arise. Other times it plans far ahead of its time.

Leonardo da Vinci must have set a world's record for creative thinking. Five hundred years ago he designed cars which needed no fuel. He built miniature grain harvesters. He had a need to create.

Who created the first contact lens for the human eye? Da Vinci, five centuries before it was marketable! Who designed the first parachute? Da Vinci, 500 years before there was an airplane.

Da Vinci's creative mind was mothered by the needs of his day. It was nurtured by the things he wanted to improve. His creativity was nursed by his need to express what was in his searching mind.

Where are you right now? Are there problems cascading on your head? Would you like to improve a few ideas? Would you like to create for your own satisfaction? All three situations can be solved by your own creative energy.

All problems are not solvable, but most are. Some difficulties will be corrected if you do nothing, but the vast majority will be rectified only if you put creativity into action.

Creativity can turn ugly emotions into beautiful productivity. A person gets angry at the muddy road by his house. Not content to fume and ulcerate, he gathers his neighbors. They agree to petition the city and have it paved.

Anger can also disintegrate into destruction, but the smart person elevates it to new heights of progress.

A parent found himself always frustrated when trying to put the children to bed at night. Every evening it seemed his voice and blood pressure rose to record levels.

Finally he decided to put the responsibility squarely on the children. If they did not go to bed and have the lights out at the designated time, he no longer blew. He simply wrote out a note that said, "Sue goes to bed 30 minutes early tomorrow night." If it happened again he wrote another note, listing the appropriate adjustments.

There were no more flare-ups—only calm evenings now. Frustrations turned into creativity. Creativity turned into peace.

Some situations are difficult, and it is natural to become frustrated or angry. The harm comes when these emotions are allowed to hurt other people or yourself.

What do you do when you are upset? Some people wash the car. Others work in the garden. I have a friend who does woodwork. He makes beautiful furniture when he is mad at his boss.

He has a need, and he satisfies that need in a highly constructive way.

Creative problem-solving is essential to meeting the challenges of life. The better we can do it, the better we handle surprises, twists, opportunities, and disappointments.

Our education experience is often centered on memorizing and reciting, and these are necessary elements. However, in that busy routine we may not have been encourged in problem-solving. If we do not practice creative problem-solving, we are not likely to do it well.

When a slowed-down economy hit our town, two creative friends decided to solve a dual problem: What business could they begin which would boost their incomes as well as help other middle- and lower-income citizens?

They hit upon an idea, rented a storefront, and opened a consignment business. Quickly people began bringing items they no longer needed.

Within three months the store was a beehive of activity. From day one it paid its own expenses, including salaries. Families were able to afford used appliances and household goods Mothers made added income by selling outgrown items. The owners received great satisfaction from their venture.

Try this problem-solving in your own group. Ask some open-ended questions. Venture into some subjects when you don't know what the outcome will be.

Try this as a starter problem: His name is Bob and he has been a Christian for a year-and-a-half. Before Bob was a Christian he was a barhopper. He drank a great deal, often got loud, and was a dangerous driver.

Since Bob has become a Christian, a group on campus has started asking him to give his testimony.

Bob likes to go to the bar, drink one beer, and keep an open relationship with his former friends.

The group which uses his testimony has become upset; they told Bob they could no longer use him if he frequents the bar.

What do you think Bob should do? Why? (This is a true story.)

Let your group, family, or class solve this problem. Refuse to give your opinion. Let them practice working it through.

If you are going to encourage this type of exercise, pick genuinely difficult situations. A problem with an obvious solution is not a problem at all. An exercise with only one possible conclusion is not enough challenge in this area.

Creativity is a risky business, but those who encourage reasonable risks will benefit enormously.

Many marriage separations have flunked creative problem-solving. An immense problem mushroomed between two individuals, then became a dragon which they could not slay. They couldn't see over, under, or around it. Maybe, just maybe, they didn't have enough practice in solving problems.

Every couple or family can cultivate problem-solving. Too often we believe there is an immovable brick wall. Maybe you went to a counselor but he didn't help. Frustrated, you quit instead of trying again.

Marriage is alive and dynamic; it responds to innovation. Here is a problem for experiment: Suppose a wife wants a full-time job outside the home. Her husband is flatly against it. Their differences have turned to hostility. Neither can mention the subject without getting upset. If some compromise isn't reached soon, the marriage may suffer serious wounds.

Rather than perish at an impasse, they decide to create. They agree on five basic steps. 1) They set up two jars, one "for" and one "against." Notepads are placed by each. As they think of reasons, they are to write them down and place them in a jar. 2) They set a definite date to make a decision. 3) They agree to consult an outside force such as a working couple, mutual friends, or a study group. 4) Each person will present a compromise proposal by the deadline date. 5) They agree not to discuss the subject between each other during this time. Every opinion can be expressed calmly on paper.

How would you change or improve this approach? Add suggestions of your own.

One couple sets aside an hour each week to talk through any plans or problems in their family.

Often we imitate the problem-solving methods of other people, and consequently we imitate their mistakes. We should use their ideas but be creative and have the ideas fit our own situation.

Moses couldn't rule his entire nation by himself. Fortunately he was smart enough to accept Jethro's creative idea (Exodus 18). Solomon could not figure out who was the real mother of a child. By innovative wisdom he suggested that they cut the infant in half (1 Kings 3). Jesus seemed to be in a moral trap when a new twist changed the entire atmosphere for the woman caught in adultery (John 8).

We often fall because we settle for obvious solutions. For centuries, when it became dark people went to bed or lit candles. Edison said there was another way. If you wanted to travel from Missouri to California in the 1800s, it would take weeks or months. The Wright brothers had another way.

How much time do you waste beating your head against old obstacles?

There are many methods of creative problem-solving. The following are some suggested steps. Almost all plans are better than none. We spend too much time flailing in the dark. Don't do it—make a plan. This prevents problems from piling up and eventually overwhelming you.

These suggestions are not carved in stone. Make up your own. However, they are a place to start. So start.

Define your problem. We waste energy fighting the wrong problems. If your son is irritable and hard to get along with this evening, you have to deal with that problem. However, you solve little until you ask if he is getting enough sleep and enough to eat.

Perhaps your daughter won't communicate. You ask her questions and try to start a conversation. But it only causes her to withdraw. Maybe you need to spend more time creating the atmosphere and free time where she can talk when she is ready.

A man cannot lift a huge rock. What is his problem? It is obvious that he isn't strong enough. Determined to succeed, he lifts weights, takes vitamins, and gets into condition. After several months he still can't lift the rock. His thin neighbor then comes over and moves the rock with a lever. Our friend sits down and cries.

His problem was not physical but mental. Unable to lift the rock, he needed to think out the problem.

Check out your confidence. The person who says "I can't solve problems" is generally correct. If you think you can solve them, you probably will conquer most of them. The person who thinks he can do something probably will. Write that on your handkerchief. Read it each time you begin to cry.

I had a friend in college who believed he could do anything, so he built his own home (though not flawlessly). How did he build a house, get a master's degree, and land a terrific job? Not because he could do everything, but because he was willing to tackle anything.

How would this attitude change your life? Instead of leaving things unsolved, your efficiency would increase immensely.

Most creative problem-solvers believe they can solve problems. If you haven't memorized Philippians 4:13 you are definitely truant.

Be knowledgeable. If you knew how simple most problems are, you would have solved them weeks ago. We are often like the ancient Sophists: They believed in speculating but not in investigating. If a clock stopped running they would speculate on what made it quit. They would not open it because that would violate their code.

I know almost nothing about car engines. I do not look at them or listen to their purr. However, sometimes I have been surprised to learn I could fix a simple part. In order to do that I had to open the hood and look at the motor.

Facing the problem is essential to problem-solving. This is simple but often ignored. We don't know what's wrong and therefore we don't know what can be done about it.

You are afraid to panel your basement. A discussion with the salesman at the hardware store would help you. You don't know how to control your rowdy class. Talking to teachers and reading suggestions might help enormously.

We do not solve problems that we do not face. We do not solve them until we find out something about them.

Flood your problem with ideas. A pencil and paper may be all it takes to turn most things around. While you are planning a job change, a move, a divorce, a resignation, or a confrontation, you may merely lack a pencil and paper.

Fifteen minutes of jotting down ideas may greatly surprise you.

Try it with your family. Present this problem to them after you have given paper and pencils to each. Don't leave the young ones out; they don't know what "won't work" and are therefore free to think clearly.

This is your problem: A family of six has planned a one-week vacation. If they had 200 dollars more they could stay a second week. How could the family pool its resources and get the money?

You have opened the gates and allowed ideas to flow. If your mind is not tied down, there could be several productive solutions.

Today's children are smart. They are idealistic and adventuresome. Don't write them off.

Letting ideas float freely through your mind is only of limited value. You are liable to forget some rare gems. Forgotten, they may never return. Write them down. Even write down wild, ridiculous ideas. What sounds absurd at first may later turn out to be the ticket you actually needed.

Don't believe everything you hear. During the 1940s and 1950s most people doubted that a man could walk on the moon.

If you believe all the people who say it can't be done, the result is fossilization. Those who have brought change have believed there was a different and better way.

To be a problem-solver does not mean that you have to be an authority on the subject. Those who are authorities are often blinded by their knowledge.

Don't anticipate the solution. If you drop a ball, what will it do? But is there a ball which does not fall when released? If there is, what else might it do? Now your mind has started to reach out to other possibilities.

Set a time to reach a conclusion. Those who dream and scheme forever are going no place. Sometimes there is merit in putting things off. However, if you wait too long the ideas degenerate. You lose your perspective. The edge turns dull.

Make a decision. If you put it off indefinitely, you could be desperately sorry.

What are the mountains you would like to conquer? Are they pressing and urgent? Are they useful and progressive? Are they fun and for your own amusement? Whichever the case, you need to put creative problem-solving to work for your benefit and for others.

Need is the mother of creativity.

Exercise

1. Susie drops food on the floor when she eats. How would you solve this problem?
2. Your house has two parents, three children, and two bedrooms. How would you arrange sleeping and other areas for privacy?
3. Your teenage girl has stopped communicating. What can you do to solve this problem?
4. Wendy is a lady who comes to your house practically every afternoon when you are starting to prepare dinner. Name four things you could do to resolve this.
5. Your family is noisy and unpleasant at mealtime. How could you improve this?
6. Your elderly parent lives with you. How can you give proper time to him and also arrange some evenings to be alone with your spouse?

Chapter Six

When to Quit

"I'd really like to do that but I just don't have the time." Thus reads the headstone over the grave of dead creativity.

I spoke to a ladies' group at their annual meeting recently. They hadn't assigned a topic, so I selected quitting. For 20 minutes I explained all the benefits of being a good quitter. Afterward the sweet president came to me gasping, "I don't know what you've done. We have so much trouble getting officers. Our group may just be finished."

Maybe that group needed to expire. Maybe they had been sapping good creative energy long enough. They might find a new freedom by cutting the threads from their wings and beginning to fly.

How many dead horses are you riding? They are going no place. If you are going to get anything significant done, you must have enough common sense to jump off.

It is stimulating to hear so much about winning, optimism, and setting new records. The air is thick with sermons promoting drive and courage without wavering. Cheers! But there are also merits in a sanctified "I quit."

The doctrine of eternal optimism can become as absurd as any extreme. Are you patching and repairing your old house when maybe it is time to move on? Does your car require so much fixing that it would be wiser to get rid of it?

Eternal optimism can become the death knell to genuine progress. There must come that moment of truth when a committee of men face each other and say, "This isn't working anymore; why don't we give it up and try something else?"

What would have happened if Abraham Lincoln had gone on to become president of Rail Splitters, Inc.? Today Billy Graham might be a state representative for Fuller Brush, D.L. Moody the founder of Moody Shoe Institute, and Bob Hope the manager of a gymnasium in Cleveland. On the road to tremendous happiness and success they knew when to quit.

Your creativity may be shackled by the chains of programs in which you see little purpose. When a church is loaded with outdated projects, it is incapable of creating exciting new ministries. Energies and time must be thrown into the relevant.

Even God quit. After man had been around a long time, God gave up on mankind except for eight warm bodies (Genesis 6:5-7). The patient Creator had had enough.

To see what happens when this principle is violated, try to recall some people who didn't have enough sense to quit. Think about the king who led his people well for 30 years but undid practically everything in his last five senile years. Remember the employee who did a fantastic job until he stayed six months too long. Recall the fine leader in the club who should have quit one term sooner. The tragedy is that many people never rise to their potential because they are afraid to leave what they have.

In a large Midwestern city there is a renowned neurosurgeon who had once been a nightclub singer, but at age 26 he decided to quit singing and study medicine. Mark Hatfield was a teacher who became an excellent politician. Somewhere there is a struggling lawyer who could be extremely happy as a plumber. All he needs is a green light to tell him it's okay to quit.

Paul knew when to quit. Remember him climbing over the wall to escape? When the nonbelievers decided to kill Paul, he quit Damascus and headed for Jerusalem. He is the same one who wrote, "I can do all things through Christ who strengthens me."

Jesus knew when to back off. Caiaphas,

the high priest, prophesied that Jesus should die on behalf of the whole nation, and a plot was made to kill Him. From that day on, Jesus no longer walked among the Jews; instead He retreated to Ephraim (John 11:54).

This isn't a campaign to get everyone to quit. Nor do I intend to open the Quitters Hall of Fame. The real purpose is to consider some of the horrendous damage done by the philosophy of "never quit."

There are some vacation centers which had their heyday 40 to 60 years ago, but now both their facilities and their programs are disasters. They refuse to become innovative and they lack the courage to give up. Administrators merely sit around chatting over the good old days.

It is difficult to quit. The word "quit" has the same final ring as "dead." Yet "quit" can also ring out with the sound of *joy:* He quit gambling, he quit his lawless gang, or he quit a job where he was unsuitable and miserable.

Because of our pride, we don't want our friends and relatives to call us quitters. Some of us are afraid to quit because we like the security of the status quo. Change is threatening even when it is for our own good. However, the hazards involved should lead us to caution and not paralysis.

Look at your situation. What stops you from sampling those creative ideas brewing in the back of your rich mind? What are you going to do about it?

Exercise

1. Name three things you would like to do if you could.
2. Name three things you should give up.

Chapter Seven

A New Attitude

People who are bedrock complainers can scarcely venture into the creative arena. If we see life as a dirty deal we are in no position to reap its benefits. A creative mind flourishes in a grateful attitude. The creative person is thankful for the rich opportunities of life and can hardly wait to get at them.

Life is made up of small keys. Its richness does not come from gigantic events but rather from common attributes. Smiles, thoughtfulness, self-acceptance, memories, touching, listening, and thankfulness are the real ingredients that make it worthwhile.

One of those rich surprises came to us during Christmas week a few years ago. It was a small thing that wouldn't make the newspapers. We didn't write home to tell our relatives. Nevertheless it was warm and moving, and it made us tremendously grateful.

Shopping, running to the post office, and gobbling down hamburgers have never been our idea of fun. This was one of those hectic days as we dashed to the car with our minds racing in different directions. When we opened the car door we were startled by the sight on the front seat.

There sat a box with a robust frozen turkey perched on top. We took the generous gift inside the house and unpacked it. Everything was there for one complete meal—two cans of corn, a large jar of cranberry juice, a bottle of olives, and everything else necessary.

Who was the kind friend who dropped this off? We looked for a note, a card, a name. We picked up each piece and searched diligently. There was no card, no name, no clue.

Pat and I sat down, smiles stretched wide, and tried to guess who had been so thoughtful. Was it our neighbor? Maybe someone at the church? Possibly a member of our little club? A couple of our close friends?

Then it dawned on us what was happening. Without even trying, my wife and I came up with a dozen names of people who might have done this. Our lives were surrounded with people who were kind enough to do something like this.

It made us thankful to be reminded that there

are so many good people. To this day we don't know who the Santa Claus was. I hope whoever it was will read this story and accept my greatest gratitude. That person did far more for us than merely give us food. His or her gift still lives today and keeps expanding.

Every once in a while I sit in a room and look at a friend across the way and think to myself, "I wonder if he or she left that meal?" And every time I think that I feel better inside.

Our mysterious friends made us thankful. They made us remember how many good and kind people God has sprinkled all around His world.

That uncluttered fact comes in handy on some of the dimmest days. It helps me forget the driver who beeped his horn and shook his fist. It helps erase the ugly words someone said when I tried to lend a hand. Those experiences will freeze us in a hurry. They make us think life is twisted, painful, and senseless. Acts of quiet kindness can help us see life as healthy, worthwhile, and satisfying.

Whoever put the food in our car committed a creative act of generosity. It in turn made us thankful and caused us to look for creative ways to do something similar. We then began to plan little surprises for other people. Generosity gave birth to thankfulness. Thankfulness in turn gave birth to greater creativity.

Gratitude lifts life from disappointment and moves it into exciting anticipation.

All of us know that life is packed with generous

portions of the uglies as well as the beautiful. Only a dimwit pretends that life is a garden of ripe cherries waiting to be picked. Both the beautiful and the ugly exist, and both leave their marks.

The great problem comes when we become lopsided. For some odd reason many of us allow our minds to tilt toward the ugly, the disappointing, and the sad. Our setbacks seem to loom over us like dark clouds threatening daily.

That's one of the reasons why I started my "Rose" file. My mind is warped in a downhill tilt. I remember insults, losses, failures, and broken glasses in livid color. I memorize mistakes. Then I dwell on them and keep them alive for years.

At the same time I seem to have a peculiar ability for rejecting successes. When I do something correctly, my mind seems to knock the memory down, drown it, and throw it out.

This attitude strangles creativity. We exaggerate failures and ignore successes. The result is a reluctance to try new, colorful adventure. We spend too much time nursing wounds to dare create again.

Several years ago I took some concrete steps toward countering this trend. I decided it was time to make my straggling mind work *for* me instead of against me. I looked for a creative solution.

The "Rose" file is a special drawer in my desk. Whenever someone sends me a "thank you" or any written compliment I read it over carefully, bask in it thorougly, and then place it gingerly in the "Rose" file.

My collection of notes isn't that great, but they are there. Occasionally I take them out and read them over again. People have been generous. They have taken time to show appreciation for little things, and I am grateful.

It's possible that not everyone's mind needs this promotional campaign; some people stay on top quite well, and others become conceited by preserving roses. However, many others of us need to marshal an army to fight despair and negativism. Any program that doesn't become extreme can be well worth the work.

Thankfulness is an attitude that we need to pass around like smiles. Thankfulness is also something we need to collect, store, and preserve for the cold nights when life takes a bum turn.

One of the things we notice about God in the Bible is His willingness to accept gratitude. He doesn't blush, rub his toe in the sand, or turn away. Thankfulness is healthy. Thankfulness is natural. Thankfulness is a high gift designed to give life meaning.

People express, accept, and promote gratitude because they can see its fantastic benefits.

"So that I might sing glad praises to the Lord instead of lying in silence in the grave, O Lord my God, I will keep on thanking you forever!" (Psalm 30:12 TLB).

Our lives are well lined with rich reasons to thank God. Some of us will be fortunate enough to take count of them and realize that it's a great day to be thankful.

Each of us has had a dismal day when everything has gone wrong. However, even in those times there are more reasons to be grateful that we at first realize.

There was an especially gloomy day when I thought things were running straight into the ground. I was driving home on a wintry evening when the roads had slicked over with an ice cover. There is a terribly dangerous dogleg curve on Route 281 in Nebraska, and the slightest storm will send snow whipping across the road.

On this day the curve was more than I could handle, and my car went into a spin. Fortunately, there was no traffic in the other lane so I made two beautiful loops before tearing off two road markers and sliding gracefully into a ditch.

When the car settled softly into the snow I counted my bones and found myself and the vehicle in good shape. The only casualties were my pride and my time.

As I sat there waiting for help the most amazing scene started to unfold. A man stopped and told me he would tell the police to send a truck. The police were so close that I could see them helping someone else less than a mile away.

Soon a second person came and I waved him on. Two men pulled up and took out a huge chain but I waved them on too. Before long 13 different people had stopped to see if they could help! I was totally surprised at how many people were willing to get involved.

Finally a police car drove up and the patrolman told me he was going to stop people from trying to help. The road was too dangerous and he was afraid someone would cause an accident. The officer stationed his car on the highway and let his red lights blink until the truck could get to me.

Imagine this: A state patrolman standing guard because too many people wanted to help! They weren't robbing me or threatening my life. Complete strangers were taking risks because they cared. This actually happened on a modern highway in America!

This story is not unique. Our days are filled with unusual kindnesses. They are sprinkled with ugly encounters too, but there are far more acts of graciousness than we have been willing to admit.

This is a great day to be thankful. This is a fantastic day to recall all the good that has happened to us, and to thank God for it.

Like creativity, thankfulness is a conscious act. It may not come naturally to all of us. However, when someone begins to practice a piano, he is likely to play better. When someone cooks, his culinary arts will probably improve.

There is an art to thankfulness that grows with practice. It raises our consciousness and allows us to see more good.

In the long run gratitude will change our personality. We will be transformed from an uptight, suspicious person into a trusting, accepting, appreciating individual—all through the magic of thankfulness.

We become thankful for the materials of life. Health, energy, freedom, resources, and enthusiasm are each magnificent gifts. By being grateful for them we become free to rearrange them in satisfying, creative ways.

The Bible tells us to pour out our thanksgiving toward God. What does God want with my feeble praise? He has galaxies, robins, giant whales, and soaring eagles. He wants us to thank Him for many reasons, but one important one occurs to me: Maybe, just maybe, God wants us to give thanks because He knows how good it is for us! When we unwind and admit that some excellent things have come our way, life blossoms.

Soon we will no longer be controlled by the bleak news poured out over television, radio, and the newspaper. We can begin to see so many bright and encouraging facets to life.

There is a twinkle that begins to form in our eyes. A bounce reappears in our steps. There is an anticipation for a terrific day. We have begun to thank God.

Now we are free, no longer bound by grouchiness, no longer victims of life. We take the creative initiative because we are grateful for life and all its great gifts.

Exercise

1. Start a "thank you" list. Write down a few things that you can thank God for. Tomorrow

add two things to the list.
2. Once a week ask everyone at the dinner table to express something they are thankful for.
3. Send more "thank you" notes and cards. They make you and the recipient feel better and help spread a feeling of happiness.

Chapter Eight

Creative Laughter

Among people who score high in creative skills one attribute keeps coming to the top: Most creative people have a sharp sense of humor. Those who have the most trouble letting go and laughing probably have difficulty letting go and creating. Read that sentence again.

Why is humor so important? First, a creative person cannot be afraid to laugh at himself. If everything has to be neat and proper, his odds of doing things differently are small. Second, he must be willing to take chances. If he is rigidly afraid to gamble, you can count him out. Third, he has to see life just a little crooked. He sees the strange angle. He thinks of things backward, upside down, and slightly lopsided. In short he sees life from a funny perspective.

Where has creative humor gone? For example, I think the military academy at West Point should be closed immediately. A special commission reported in an official communique that the school's administration was guilty of losing its sense of humor. We shouldn't ignore this accusation. It is a high crime.

The distrust of humor is apparently an adult ailment. We all laughed more as children. Remember the old comedies where someone had a pie thrown in his face? We rolled with laughter like otters on a snowslide. But now we are grown up. Life is terribly serious. Do you know how much it costs to get pie stains out of a suit?

Adults aren't too old to enjoy being goofy. The next time you want to send a postcard to get someone's attention, head for the local pizza store. For loose change you can buy a round cardboard the size of a large pizza. Write your message on one side and put the address of your sweetheart, boss, or city councilman on the other. For less than a dollar you can grab someone's attention and a few laughs at the same time.

Laughter is a bona fide emotional need. Anyone who gives it up for the serious side has an area of his life that is starving to death.

A creative family looks for ways to celebrate — any excuse to get together and laugh from the bottoms of their toes. When your daughter gets accepted into college, when your son wins the two-mile, when your youngster performs in a musical, it's time to celebrate. Break out the ice cream, pile up a bowlful of candy, sit on the floor, and be silly. These are happy times. Life will bring enough sadness on its own. It's our job to reach out and make the laughter.

Sometimes the more serious the subject the more humor is called for. A hospital chaplain made this observation about death: He thought that families who faced death best were the ones with the best humor. They could remember the times they had laughed together. Their memories were happy ones. Those who treated life as dreadfully serious were facing still another stern reality.

Laughter adds the surprises that make life interesting. One day I gave one of the girls a ride to her piano lesson. When we stopped at the teacher's door I asked her to carry in three large cardboard boxes. I explained that the teacher needed them and we would be grateful.

The only thing I failed to tell her was that it was April Fool's Day and that anything might happen. By the time it was over she knew it was all right to have a sense of humor.

A balanced sense of humor is an investment in good health. There is no way to calculate how many ulcers and heart attacks might have been avoided by a few hearty laughs—something to cut the tension and relieve the pressure. Abraham Lincoln said, "With the fearful strain that is on me night and day if I did not laugh, I should die."

Science Digest has listed a number of healthy results from laughter. It expands the lungs and clears the respiratory system. Laughing gives us a wholesome outlet for emotions and a good avenue for extra energy. It's an excellent solution for boredom, shyness, tension, and worry.

Dr. Jacob Levine, professor of clinical psychology at the Yale School of Medicine, believes we can tell a great deal about mental health from laughter. People who see humor in life have probably made a better adjustment to their environment. When every part of life poses a threat it has to be a painful journey.

This doesn't mean we have to develop a horse laugh or slap people on the knee every time. Laughter might be a few chuckles or a warm feeling inside. It is the attitude that really registers.

When a recent U.S. president was in deep trouble, news commentators were pouring on their complex analyses. One reporter cut through the verbiage and summed up the situation curtly, "The President's problems are fatal—he has lost his sense of humor."

It isn't easy to laugh when we take ourselves so seriously. The school administrator thinks his role is most important. The doctor sees his service as the backbone of life. English teachers are convinced that poor communication is the cause of national catastrophies and the demise of the civilized world. A lawyer believes he represents the essence of freedom and liberty. Some advertising executives imagine they are the reason why capitalism remains intact.

No wonder some of these groups have the highest suicide rates in the country! The simple fact is many of us have grossly overestimated our importance. We tend to be so dreadfully serious.

We owe ourselves the gift of laughter. It is essential to give ourselves time out to be silly. Laughter will cut tension and free our minds to see the ridiculous.

Not everything in life is funny. It's hard to laugh with a boil growing on a strategic place of our anatomy. Some things hurt desperately. Others have to be handled with intense sobriety. That is all the more reason to laugh while we are able. Times will come soon enough when we would like to smile but can't.

There are few things as personal as laughter. No one can make us laugh. Unless someone tickles us we can remain stoic as long as we want to. There are no physical reflexes which have to respond to a funny situation. We can smother humor if we choose. When an individual sees all of life as a grim, serious business, he is saying more about himself than about life. He could find some things to smile about, but he doesn't want to.

I know a man who has lost two children in death. He has ample reason to see life as a tough taskmaster. Yet the man has chosen to carry the most pleasant sense of humor. It isn't overworked and doesn't smack of pretending. He garners the genuinely funny twists to life. Mixed with his faith in God, he enjoys even the strange contradictions of those who take themselves so seriously.

It would be safe to say that offices, clubs, businesses, factories, and families run more smoothly because we can laugh at each other. Watch two people who are having trouble communicating. A tension hovers over their heads. They don't know how seriously to take each other. Is the other person joking or trying to insult you? Things that would normally bounce lightly off your chest crush painfully into your ribs. In such a rigid atmosphere misunderstanding and frayed nerves are inevitable. Like a train in the distance, you know it is only a matter of time.

Compare that with a group that has parties, celebrates even small occasions, and appreciates a good joke in its place. These are people who can live and work together better.

Laughter is a key ingredient even for those who do not speak the same language. One lady tells of her frustrations in trying to help a Laotian mother and wife. Trying to explain taxes, insurance, driving laws , and gas bills is difficult in any tongue. Often totally frustrated at trying to explain a word or justify an American custom, the two would finally roll on the floor laughing until they cried. Everything appeared so important, and yet it was so silly at the same time. They could handle life's absurdities better because they could laugh at them.

If history is so serious it might be dangerous for you to experiment with a creative way to teach it. If all of medicine is crucial then no one dare touch its ancient taboos. If education is everything we had better take no risks and make classes boring, dull, and safe. Those who do not take life this seriously look at it from a slightly crooked angle and can make it better.

A gentleman donated a copy machine to his favorite club. For some reason known only to him the price tag was left on the handle. A stir arose across the membership. Why did he do it? Should they accept the gift?

Before the episode was over the club split down the middle. One half dropped out. However, neither the copy machine nor the man caused the group to split. The reason was their lack of a sense of humor. People weren't able to laugh away the problem.

People who are not afraid of humor are frequently more open-minded, easy going, and creative. It is not merely a helpful ingredient, but in most cases it is vital. Those who take life too seriously are usually afraid to try anything new. Since they can't handle the thought of failing, they decide to play life safely.

The Bible has a bright way of saying things. The author of Proverbs understood the principle: "A cheerful heart does good like medicine, but a broken spirit makes one sick" (17:22 TLB).

Exercise

1. When was the last time you laughed at yourself? Give the time and the situation.
2. If you could do one funny thing, what would it be?
3. Name one thing you should never do on a honeymoon.
4. Give three uses for crunched typing paper.

Chapter Nine

Creative Faith

Faith includes the hope of heaven, a new world, and collections of angels. However, this is only one facet of faith. It is also made up of paper clips, radio waves, light bulbs, and mosquito repellent.

The person who wants a new ceiling in his living room has to exercise faith. He believes the ceiling will look good. He can picture himself putting it up piece-by-piece. He may have some fears about his ability, but he charges forward. The weekend carpenter then watches his hope become reality: Existing materials are compiled into a dream come true.

This isn't a low view of faith; it is a high one. To restrict faith solely to ecclesiastical matters is insulting to God. Faith involves shoes, food, careers, track meets, and love.

Secular faith is used daily by our associates. Someone borrows money to launch a career. Two people get married fully believing that their union will work like trained acrobats. A neighbor sends in a patent for a cottage cheese cooler. Without faith they would each shut down and give up.

Not too long ago you probably committed an act of pure faith. Your doctor handed you a piece of paper called a prescription. It appeared to you that no man, beast, or Martian could hope to read it.

Dutifully you handed it to your druggist. Soon he handed you 30 tiny green pills to be swallowed, one after each meal. You obeyed without raising the slightest protest.

You accepted the medicine by faith and it did its job. But do not mistake the process: Each step was one of exercising faith in a fairly common part of life.

William Mitchell was a chemist for General Foods for over 35 years. During that time he patented over 50 items. Mitchell develped a process to extract pectin from oranges. This little miracle earned 10 million dollars for the company.

He also happened to place a small dose of carbon dioxide inside candy capsules. Management toyed with Mitchell's new idea but thought costs were excessive and the market uncertain. For 20 years the idea waited. Finally, after two decades, Pop Rocks came on the market. Mitchell had faith in a product and went on to see that faith work.

Faith does not mean that everything will work. If faith meant that everything would work, it would cease to be faith and become fact.

Someone says, "If I had enough faith in God I could become wealthy." Not so. "If I claimed a large corporation to the glory of God I could get it." Nonsense.

If there is no risk, there is no faith. Anyone can try something if the outcome is guaranteed. Faith and risk are first cousins. So are faith and creativity.

It takes almost no faith to copy or trace. If I go swimming I incorporate only minimal faith. However, the first person who did it expended a ton of faith.

The greater the risk you take, the greater the faith you need. Rocking on the porch is a low-faith operation.

Ask yourself this question and learn a great deal about yourself: Is faith mostly the ability to stand still or the ability to try change?

Both may be an experience in faith, but there is a tremendous difference. The first is a holding operation; it usually takes little imagination and practically no creativity. It is short-armed and defenseless.

The second is bold, reaching, and adventuresome.

A Biblical description of faith best fits the second approach: "Faith is being sure of what we hope for and certain of what we do not see. This is what the ancients were commended for" (Hebrews 11:1 NIV).

They were applauded for reaching out for things they had never seen before.

To experience the faith of creativity we must be willing to stretch. We *will* reach out. We *will* venture where we have previously been reluctant to roam.

If secular or common faith is productive, how much more can Christian faith be? Four dentists in a large city stepped from the realm of secular faith into the exciting arena of Christian faith. Each year one of these partners travels to a mission field for 12 months and does dental work. Revolving in this manner is a risky business. How well will they fit into another culture? Will it hurt their practice to be gone? Is it reasonable to expect the other three men to make money for them while they are away?

This is a clear case of applied creativity by faith in Christ.

Could this project have fallen through? Of course! Faith does not make things risk-proof. Faith merely gives the courage to try in the face of incredible odds.

The principle applies if you are opening a hotel chain, going out for the basketball team, or agreeing to tutor a slow learner. Faith gives the courage to try.

A Christian is able to take risks that other

people might not consider. He will go to college at age 35. He will contribute heavily to a good cause. He will serve on a board. A vivacious Christian has the added ingredient of faith in Jesus Christ.

With this prospect the amazing thing is that we don't attempt more!

There is a doctor in our town who dropped out of college after two years. He traveled back to the farm and decided to break sod the rest of his life. After six years away from the academic world he changed his mind. He went back to college, then to medical school. To muster up the courage to go again he had three essentials: He had faith in God, faith in himself, and a terrific wife.

A non-Christian could have done what he did. Many do. However, this man was able to use the extra strength at his disposal and tap his Christian faith.

God is saying to us, "Tell me what you have in mind. Just what new, interesting, creative goal would you like to aim for?" After you explain it to Him, He will send it through His majestic computer. He will weigh factors that we have never considered. He will see the entire picture. He alone can check out time as well as circumstances. If everything adds up He will help you reach your goal.

I think this is what God is saying in Matthew 7:8-10: "For everyone who asks, receives. Anyone who seeks, finds. If only you will knock, the door will open. If a child asks his father for a loaf of bread, will he be given a stone instead? If he asks for a fish, will he be given a poisonous snake? Of course not!" (TLB).

Can you picture God as alert, searching, and experimental? Do you see Him as filled with new ideas and just waiting to see some of His people try them?

How we picture God's attitude toward creativity will to a large extent influence our own attitude.

A community of believers live in Bloomington just outside Minneapolis. Forty years ago several businessmen prayed about an idea. They were successful at what they were doing, but they wanted to expand their abilites to serve Christ more directly.

By creative faith the men sold their homes and bought land together. Each took a small allowance but otherwise decided to give all they could earn to the work of Christ.

Today this community has grown and includes several factories, a publishing house, and a college. The Bethany Fellowship has given over a million dollars to missions. It began by faith because some Christians were not afraid to dream.

I belong to a writer's guild. Each person has a seed of an idea and an enormous mountain looming over him. How can he catapult over that obstacle and land safely in the arms of a loving editor?

The odds against him are stupendous. If he sends a manuscript to a large publishing house, his prospects of publication are approximately 2500 to one.

And yet the members of the guild try. As a result some succeed—an article here, a book there.

Faith is the willingness to try, to reach out for things you have never held before, to imagine scenes you have never seen. Faith is as simple as that.

The things you practice in life usually become easier to do. The hobby you spend time on, you will probably master. Creative faith needs time and effort.

When was the last time you did something by faith when you didn't have to? Praying for a sick child doesn't count. Praying to pass an exam is disqualified. Both may be valid but they were done under pressure.

My friend did it this way: A special offering was going to be taken for a family in distress. Fire had destroyed their home and most of their possessions. In three weeks a collection would be taken to help them.

This young Christian had a family, and like most of us he was broke. He simply had no money. His first impulse was to forget it. Yet he felt such concern for the family that he told himself he would try. While talking to God and no one else he promised to place 60 dollars in the offering on the designated Sunday.

A couple of days later his boss asked him if he could work that evening. It gave him 15 dollars extra. Soon he received a refund he had long forgotten. When the time for the offering came he had the 60 dollars he had promised God by faith.

He also built a foundation in exercising creative faith. The next time it will be a little easier.

There is something in us which imagines that faith and creativity belong to other people. We love to hear testimonies, but creativity is ours to claim. Daring, inventiveness, and imagination are all common qualities. The decision to use them is ours. Launch out on something. Don't be content to read about other people.

Not every story of creative faith is one of prosperity. Too often the approach is "If you love God, you'd be rich." This is too narrow a view. Words like *sacrifice, give,* and *distribute* are still a large part of the gospel.

Think of the family who says, "Let's not go to Denver next weekend. We could give the money to the Hunger Foundation. If we use our imagination we could have a great time right here." If we sacrifice that which costs us nothing, it cannot be a sacrifice (2 Samuel 24:24).

One of the richest words in the English language is *audacity.* It divides the capable person who merely dreams from the capable person who accomplishes.

A young man was talking about a football player at the university. He said, "I don't understand. I played with the guy in high school. Frankly, I never thought he could play better than I could."

What was the difference between the two? Audacity. One showed up for training camp. The other didn't have enough faith in himself. The one talking may well have been the better player, but he failed to mix it with audacity.

If we have an adequate faith and a healthy audacity, Christian creativity will take a marked direction. We will find ways to benefit other people with what we create. When operated at its best, creative faith cannot be a selfish scheme.

Do you feel you don't have much faith? I don't either. Christ told us that it takes only a mustard seed of faith to move a mountain (Matthew 17:20).

Generally the problem is not our lack of faith; more often it is our reluctance to use what we have.

Many scientists made fun of George Washington Carver's research methods, but they could not laugh at his results. When he wanted to find uses for the peanut, he locked himself in his laboratory. For days he experimented and talked to God. God not only responded but made Carver the father of synthetics.

Too many of us have padded ourselves with excuses. The young want to try creative faith after they "live a little." The middle-aged intend to try it once their "family is raised." The elderly can't try it because they are "tired." We will never know what we have missed!

Bonnie decided to aim for college. She had the ability but not the money. She talked to God and packed her bags.

In college Bonnie picked up odd jobs here and there. She received a few dollars as gifts. Four years later Bonnie graduated and looked back to see where she had been. During her education over 10,000 dollars had come to her from one source or another!

Faith is the ability to launch out when you cannot guarantee the outcome. Abraham had this kind of faith when he left for a land he had never seen. He was content because God would go with him.

Most of the time faith seems to hibernate. It is alive but sleeping. Faith's temperature has dropped drastically, and we are living off stored fat. Spring comes, but instead of waking up we decide to sleep all year round.

Faith has the potential to see things that other people cannot imagine. Creative faith conjures up hope where others see only despair. Faith is mobility.

Christopher Columbus put several ingredients together. He *believed* he would not fall off the earth. He *believed* he was a capable captain who could find the unfound. He *believed* God could use the voyage to bring good news to the heathen. Those who did not *believe* stayed home and guessed what might happen.

Exercise

1. Name the last thing you did by faith which you did not have to do.
2. Plan one action you are willing to try by creative faith.
3. When will you begin your act of creative faith? Give a date.
4. Name one activity you have long wanted to do. Why haven't you done it? What can you do about it now?

Chapter Ten

Teaching Our Children

Children are naturally creative. They don't have to take classes or study the theory of creativity. Each child is curious, innovative, and open.

Unfortunately, as he grows and finds that creativity is frowned upon, he begins to withdraw. Finally he no longer cares to stretch and dream.

Hopefully you are reading this chapter because you think something can be done about that. Your child does not have to be packaged that way.

Creativity is hope. Creativity is the developing

dream for tomorrow. Creativity is the chance for your child to reach his amazing potential.

Whenever a society has degraded creativity, the result has been stagnation and decay. The fourteenth century with its disease, superstition, and lack of progress is a prime example.

The United States during the past hundred years has been a trophy to energies of creativity. We have freed ourselves from sweatshops, child labor, and most starvation because we have prized the creative life. Cotton gins, airplanes, automobiles, assembly lines, ballpoint pens, and computers have joined constructive hands to make our standard of life possible. Our future love for creativity will in large part determine what tomorrow will be like.

Creativity has also contributed tremendously to the outreach of the church. An enormous publishing industry, mass media, and innovative ministries have all helped in an effective outreach.

That creative genius Albert Einstein said it well: "Making allowance for human imperfections, I do feel that in America the most valuable thing in life is possible, the development of the individual and his creative powers."

Your children are going to be part of a growing, leaping tomorrow. Whatever their career, their future will be filled with inventive ideas. Do them a favor and help them get ready.

My optometrist tells me of a machine on the market which will test eyes by computer. The patient sits behind it and a technician merely pushes a button. By tracing the curvature of your eye, it will immediately register your reading vision. In another use of computers, law enforcement officers can check your license number with the FBI without getting out of their cars.

Our children will need to accept new ideas rapidly. They will also need to explore and produce in a fast-changing world. They will thank you for preparing them for a creative tomorrow.

There are two basic steps in helping children develop their creativity. First, we need to release and encourage what they can already do. Second, we need to teach them to reach into areas they might not have thought possible.

What type of model do you furnish for your child? It is unfair to expect our children to rise above us. It does happen, but it is unfair to expect it.

Often a child will become a good carpenter if the father is one. Part of this is innate ability, but he also had an excellent model to follow. He picked up attitudes, watched performance, and listened to words of approval.

Parents who are authoritarian are frequently wet blankets to creativity. There is no room for reaching, searching, and curiosity. To challenge any idea or thought is to invite all-out war. The child finds it easier to think like the person in control.

In elementary school my son had a wild teacher. Not content to stand still, the teacher occasionally walked across the tabletops. He played cards during class, had too many recesses, and kidded with the students. Result: Jim enjoyed school and his interests widened. Discipline? No problem. Who would want to get the teacher angry?

An open environment produces an open child. A closed environment is likely to shut a child down.

Look at yourself. The children around you will become amazingly like you. You cannot lead a dull, routine life while hoping they will rise up to creativity. You are like gravity. Your behavior and attitude will tend to hold them where you are.

The most creative present you can give the children around you is a creative example.

Children are extremely creative during their first few years. When school begins the boys appear to be more creative than the girls. At approximately the fourth grade both sexes have shut down rather drastically.

What happened? First, they ran out of models. Second, they ran out of rewards.

They ran out of models because the world began to become dreadfully serious and demanding. Parents led grinding, busy lives and teachers were not daring and exploring. Friends started conforming like tin soldiers, and so they did too.

After the fifth and sixth grades a few children will try their wings at individuality again, but most will not. It is painful to go upstream.

A few leaders like yourself protest. "Don't collapse into mediocrity. Don't be rocked into a monotonous sleep. Your mind is too young to fossilize into the routine. Follow me. We will create. We will dare. We will explore!"

Closely related to modeling is reward. What reward do your children receive for being creative? Think of reward in the broadest sense. When Junior sets the table with all the dishes on one side of the table, do you say, "That's a neat idea. Let's try it"? When sister turns out the lights and puts on candles, or when mother spreads out the tablecloth on the floor to eat Oriental-style, is your reaction enthusiasm?

Our face, voice, and motions send out messages. Creativity grows best in a welcoming attitude.

A smile, a "Thank you," a simple " That's a good idea" are appreciated rewards.

Three cheers for our local school. They have a creative problem-solving class in which the students explore areas that challenge their greatest potential. The student feels that he is important in the class. His opinions and ideas are helpful. He has a voice in solving the problem. The teacher is willing to deal with the answers wherever they lead. Creative solutions are encouraged.

Try it with a group of adults. Give a class a problem and divide them into couples. The couple with the most original and practical solution can be designated the winner. How can we help single, poor mothers? Elderly people confined to wheelchairs? Foreign students with language problems? Slow learners in kindergarten? Parents with a handicapped child? Older people who need help with their home or yard? A retired schoolteacher who can't drive anymore?

Inspire your children to think of original gifts to make for their grandmother. Have them write down five new ideas for camping. Sponsor your own "creativity fair."

On several occasions we have made up a worship service at home. Each person was responsible for five to ten minutes of the service.

One person would play a hymn on the record player. Another told a story with a flannel board. A third read a chapter from the Bible. Someone else got behind a chair and led singing with a puppet. Another had a quiz.

Was it silly? Everyone learned from it and everyone participated. The time went by like a rifle shot and each person received an extra message: It's all right to be creative around here.

This is what makes charades so much fun. You can stretch your imagination like an old girdle. "Simon Says" allows a mind to free-lance.

Creativity needs materials. You can create in a barren prison cell, but it is hard. What do your children have to mold, make, bend, and twist? Is your house so neat and sterile that nothing can be moved or ventured?

Materials can be simple and available—paper and clips, crayons and erasers, boxes, cans and bricks.

Next Christmas how about 50 dollars worth of building materials? Used materials go even further. Don't specify what to build.

Maybe you will see a hideout. Possibly a race car. Your child will have both the dreams and the material to let those dreams become realities.

Material must be accompanied with opportunity. Do not program your children to death. Scouts, hockey teams, 4-H, and choir can all be beneficial, but not if they completely consume all your child's energy and free time. Creativity must have breathing room. When children are young the parents needs to regulate the amount of TV viewing time or it will become a lion which eats hours raw. When we turn the TV off there may be 15 minutes of grumbling, but then everyone finds something more creative to do.

Don't make the mistake of lifting all restrictions. Children or adults are not prepared for this. Spell out the boundaries. No, you cannot put firecrackers in the couch to see if the stuffing blows. No, you may not feed goldfish to little sis.

Boundaries will not inhibit creativity, but they might save fingers and toes. Creative children who are capable of messing up can find creative ways of cleaning up. This won't cause them to stutter either.

Aim for creativity within well-defined restraints. The opposite is merely anarchy.

Don't offer a freedom unless you mean it. If you tell your son he may go to a friend's house and use his own judgment about when to come home, don't be surprised when he comes in at midnight.

Let your child know where he may create: "You may create with your room *but* it must be neat. You may create with your clothes *but* I expect them to be clean and patched. Tell me how you think school could be improved *but* you must be polite."

Search for honest opinions from children and youth. Many of us are still suffering from the old muzzler, "Children should be seen and not heard." Push yourself to open the lines of healthy expression. Your child might have an answer to lighten your food budget. He may know exactly why your new paneling won't fit. He probably knows what two paints you have to mix to get purple. She may know how you could free up time to sew a new outfit.

Let him know that you respect his opinion. What about women holding elective office? Are drugs really a problem in school? If you were president what would be the first thing you would do?

He is watching his value rise. Someone cares about what he has to say. "Dad did change something because of me. The teacher used my suggestion." He is being encouraged to create and express those creations.

Brainstorming is a great asset with children— sitting in a room and throwing ideas around. Industry is finding it increasingly valuable, and so are households.

In brainstorming ask open-ended questions, ones for which there isn't only one answer. Help your children field the possibilities and choose a direction. They can help see the way to simplify maintenance of the house or the best use of the five vacation days.

It is especially important to ask open-ended questions when talking about faith. Then we can hear what a child is thinking and feeling.

One evening we asked our children to tell us something about Mary, the mother of Jesus. Our youngest daughter said, "She was a nun."

Anxious to know why, we asked her what made her think so. She had watched a Bible story on a black-and-white television, and Mary was wearing a dark robe which looked like a habit. Conclusion: She was a nun.

How long would she have thought that if no one had asked her about Mary?

What do your children think? What do they dream? What are they afraid of? If money were no object, what would they like to do?

We all want to mold our children, but will it be a small, tight mold? Can you picture a roomy mold with plenty of extra crevices and compartments? If the mold is wide and pleasant, your child just might reach out and fill up more than you expected.

Exercise

1. Hand out pictures from a magazine and ask each person to make up a short story to match it.
2. Suppose you could not laugh or clap your hands. What would you do to show that something was funny?

3. Agree on a problem in your house. Have each family member suggest three solutions.
4. Pick out an object. If it could sing, what song would it sing?
5. Which is more important, speed running or distance running?
6. Invent a new word to:
   a. Describe a bird flying upside-down.
   b. Name the piece of skin between your nostrils.
   c. Name a wart.

Chapter Eleven

Encouraging Others

"Pick me up," Cliff asked as he turned his back to me.

"Do what?" I asked, bewildered.

"Put your arms around me and lift me off the ground," he explained. "Then drop me."

I grabbed him in a big bear hug and pulled Cliff into the air. In less than a minute I dropped him roughly.

"Great," he said. "Do it again. My back stiffens and that seems to jar it loose."

It felt good to pick someone else up physically and try to help him. You aren't a surgeon repairing a heart valve but just giving a guy a lift. For a little while it makes his life a bit easier.

All of us want to have a good effect on other people. We want to brighten their day and if possible help them realize their potential. That is why it becomes important to encourage other people to exercise their creativity. We would hate to see our children, our spouse, or our friends fail to see their dreams come true.

Sometimes we forget how easily we control other people. When you come home after work, your first few sentences have a tremendous effect on your spouse. Most of the time you will change his or her mental barometer.

Controlling people sounds sinister and unhealthy, but it doesn't need to be. Trying to manipulate people upward is admirable. If you cheer someone who is despondent, you have done him a favor.

I once knew a grouchy editor of a newspaper. He probably had seen too many old movies, and thought editors were suppposed to be crusty and grumpy.

The editor did me a favor so I sent him a simple note of appreciation. When I later saw him on the street, his face broadened into a wide grin.

"I get a lot of notes," he smiled, "but most of them are complaints. It has been years since anyone has written to say thank you."

He had allowed people to control him without even realizing it. Daily demands, pressures, and complaints had pushed him into his shell. Stiff-necked and rough-voiced, he prepared for any storms that came whistling in.

The principle is sound and Biblical; all of us have seen it work: Begin to compliment a hostile child and often that child will begin to melt.

"You were really nice to do that."

"Thanks for keeping the ball out of my flowers."

"I'll tell your parents what a great boy you've been."

People tend to adapt to their environment. In a loud, distrustful, dissatisfied setting we all tend to blend in. Kind, accepting, grateful surroundings usually have the same effect.

When we believe someone is shy, we tend to make him that way. If we tell someone he is just an average worker, he usually fulfills the role assigned to him. If we encourage him to see himself as creative and innovative, he frequently perceives himself in that light. Most often we escape the dull because someone encouraged us to escape the dull.

The art of thanking people has miracle-working properties. We lift a person's self-esteem, we increase his expectation, and we make him feel good. This is not to say that all the world needs is a few thank yous and six or seven pats on the back and the New Jerusalem is just around the corner. However, it is to say that people affect people. Our thoughtfulness can help someone else anywhere from 1 percent to 50 percent in the reshaping of his attitude.

Today I received two letters in the mail. (The envelopes with the cellophane windows don't count.) One letter was a hefty rebuke. The other was a generous compliment. Neither letter was necessarily fair. Both letters affected me.

Fortunately the kind letter far outweighed the unpleasant one. The thankful letter helped tremendously to keep my day on a high level.

Karl Menninger calls the withholding of gratitude a serious matter. There are many people who are deeply injured simply because others are too stingy to say "thank you."

Some people unfortunately see gratitude as a sign of weakness. However, it's hard to estimate how much damage has been done merely because we have withheld recognition and appreciation. Children have had their talents ignored. Employees have been taken for granted. Spouses are treated routinely. The elderly are spoken to callously. We hold the ability to discourage people, and we also have the gift to raise them to new levels of creativity.

It's like carrying a bucket of water. As you walk along the hot, parched road, you see tired and thirsty travelers alongside. You can't give them all a drink but you can brighten the day for a few.

Sometimes it is difficult to express our sincere gratitude. There was a young man who had received a great deal from his parents. Braces, shots, shoes, and camping trips were all part of the parade that came his way. Each gift was heavily draped in healthy love.

When the boy was a young man in college, his heart was filled with appreciation for all that he had received. He wanted to tell his parents what was swelling up in his chest, but it was hard. Never having gotten into the habit of saying "thank you," it was now a high step.

Gratitude at its best aims to help other people. Thankfulness says, "I want her to know how much she helped me." Its goal is to lift up someone else.

My wife's uncle lived near the water and loved the sea. One night during a terrible storm a knock rattled urgently against his door. There stood three sailors soaked and winded. They needed to get into town but had no way to do so. The old gentleman invited them in and called a taxi. Soon the entire incident was over.

A few months later on a clear day another knock came. When he opened the door there stood two of the sailors he had helped that windy night. They wanted to know if the elderly uncle would join them on the ship and have dinner at the captain's table. They just wanted to say thank you. They couldn't have made him happier if they had crowned him King of Siam.

What a fantastic opportunity to control people! This is not a demeaning, enslaving management of lives; this is a thankfulness that picks up and doesn't put down.

Mushy, pretend gratitude can do more harm than good. Children and adults both understand a gushy put-on. It's like a forced, nervous smile. It's like a Christmas card list which a secretary grinds out each year and the boss is only vaguely aware it exists. Perfunctory, automatic, and formal thanksgiving carries a stuffy air that lacks both heart and warmth.

"We would like to thank everyone associated with this." That is one of the well-meaning, hollow statements of life. It's a little like "God bless all the children."

Compare that with a personal, handwritten note. There are few laws to govern gratitude, but sincerity and personableness are essential.

The amazing thing is that our expressions of gratitude often send other people into a flurry of creativity. A recipient of gratitude will have his imagination catch fire. Soon he will look for a fresh, innovative way to express his appreciation to others. Creativity usually begets creativity.

O.J. Simpson was a gigantic star of football ability. Each year that Simpson gained 1000 yards rushing he remembered to say thank you. He invited the entire offensive line out for a luxurious dinner. At that bash he told them personally that he couldn't have done it without them. He controlled people by lifting them up.

Paul understood how to be thankful for people and let them know how he felt: "I thank my God upon every remembrance of you" (Philippians 1:3 KJV).

It is practically impossible to lift up another person without lifting up ourselves at the same time. While we are thankful for someone, we cannot distrust, dislike, or hate that person. It's hard to spray perfume on someone without collecting some of the fragrance.

The next time we start to think about the

borish, overbearing relative, we could benefit by calling ourselves back to reality. How many reasons do we have for being thankful for that person?

Possibly we can be thankful that he helps out our elderly parents. We could be grateful for all the troubles he doesn't cause. Maybe we are glad he is not demanding and rude.

Each time we say "Thank God" for this or that feature, we have diminished our dislike for that person. Every dislike we discard sets us free to love, enjoy, and open up. When we cut chains off other people we cut chains from our own wrists.

When we dislike someone our circle of creativity shrinks accordingly. There are more people we cannot deal with, more places where we do not feel comfortable, more avenues where we are reluctant to go. The freer we are of hostilities the greater our potential to dream and see those dreams come true.

Who would you like to change, not in a mean, self-serving way but for that person's good? It can begin by pouring gratitude on him. He will become saturated with your grateful spirit. Some hard hearts can resist kindness, but not many. Most people will be transformed by our sincere, consistent thankfulness.

This simple principle applies particularly to the people living in our homes. If we would like a new spouse, a changed young person, or a refurbished child, this is one way to do it. Let him know how thankful you are for him and what he does.

Our oldest daughter and a carload of her friends packed into a booth in a local pizza palace. They were having a good time. They made noise and laughed a lot. An hour went quickly and their sides hurt from enjoying themselves.

Finally the waiter came over to bring the check, but there was none in his hand.

"Do you remember the lady in the next booth with the two small children? She was so impressed that a bunch of teenagers could have a good time and still not offend other people that she paid your bill. You don't owe a dime!"

Not one person in that booth will forget what that lady did. It will be interesting to see what creative ways they find to do something similar for other people.

Possibly you live with someone whom you feel is wasting his talent and ability. Encouragement and example can frequently have a dramatic effect on his life. However, if you choose a dull, uneventful existence it is nearly impossible to help other people soar to new heights.

Fortunately you have the potential to set the pace.

Exercise

1. Name someone who seems to be in a downward spin. How might you encourage him *today?*
2. What do you own that someone else could turn into a creative idea? Why don't you give it to him?
3. How can you stimulate someone in your home to a more creative outlook on life?

Chapter Twelve

What Is Inspiration?

Did you ever picture a poet sitting in a clover field with paper and pen? Suddenly his face begins to glow as a beautiful line floods his mind. Quickly he writes down the rare gem.

This is the idea that many people have of inspiration. Have you imagined songwriters, inventors, and military leaders being strangely inspired? Maybe some of them were, but most were not. The majority of good ideas come from hard, honest work. There are few shortcuts. This is tremendously encouraging, because it means that new and exciting ideas are within the reach of most people who work at it.

Too many people sit around waiting for a mysterious light to strike. They insist they can't do anything innovative because God has not moved them. Their waiting accomplishes nothing.

The quiet voice of God whispers in their ears, "Get up and get going."

The Bible does not know inspiration in the same sense we are using it. Only once does the word appear in the New Testament (2 Timothy 3:16). In this instance it refers only to the Scriptures.

This isn't to say that God plays no role in creative thinking. However, only the foolish sit around waiting for something to strangely move them.

A young lady says she would like to write poetry. Has she written any? No. She is waiting for the right "inspiration." She may sit until cobwebs weave a pattern in her hair. If you want to write poetry, the best way is to write poetry. If you want to invent a better kite, the best way is to begin working with kites.

George Washington Carver told the moving story of communicating with God as he worked with the peanut. I believe every word of that beautiful story. I have no doubt that God helped him tremendously. Yet it wasn't help which required no work; the entire time that Carver asked God for guidance, the scientist worked diligently.

Does God inspire the writing of books? Certainly He can't be responsible for every volume on the market. Does God inspire some of the books? That's a possibility, but who knows which ones? Unable to say that a particular idea is definitely from God, we work with an attitude of wanting Him to guide us.

All of creativity needs a generous portion of humility. It wasn't all your idea nor was it necessarily God's. We are simply grateful that we could carry it out. Being humble and thankful are at the core of a beautiful attitude.

The Bible says that every good and perfect gift comes from God. Consequently we are always grateful.

Where do good ideas come from? Each of us continues to store the information we gather. It's like a squirrel collecting nuts.

Ideas lie in wait for the time when you are prepared to use them.

That is why creative people are not afraid to expose themselves to change. Their minds are sucking up new concepts, inventions, and experiments like a vacuum. People who are suspicious and fearful of change seldom feel inspired.

The person who wants to become a dispenser of new ideas has to start at the other end. He begins by collecting. He is like a tinkerer who saves string, wire, nuts, and bolts. At the time he isn't sure how they can be used. However, when the right time comes, all the odd materials are available.

Work, read, and explore in order to make yourself a better person. Out of this vast resource will come ideas and "inspiration."

Exposure plays a large part in nurturing ideas. Here are two guidelines. First, listen to many ideas. We tend to restrict ourselves to a small range of thinking. Second, always be ready to question. With constant repetition we tend to accept some concepts without examination.

Some colleges hire only their graduates as faculty members. This is serious and dangerous inbreeding. Exposure to opposing concepts is essential.

Thinking is limited if you listen to a few ideas too often. This is what comes in much advertising. Commercials keep pumping the same themes. The important thing in life is to look good, get more gusto, own a beautiful car, join the sex chase.

When these ideas are continuously flashed at us, they become paramount. Other values are diminished or eliminated. Repeatedly pounding a few ideas excludes the wealth of other ideas.

There are two things that leave our idea bank empty: The restriction of new ideas by isolating ourselves and the constant pounding of a few ideas. Are you trapped in one or both of these boxes?

Take saying grace at the table. Many of us who do it regularly have fallen into a predictable nonthinking rut.

There are new methods and a few good time-tested ones which we have forgotten.

Have a search for ideas with your family. What are some different ways you could go about it? How about singing, saying grace at the end of the meal, saying thank You with your eyes open, or praying at one meal and having it count for all day? What suggestions can you come up with? Innovation may bring life. Give it a chance.

There is also an area where knowledge gives birth to new concepts. If we know the many diversified ways in which something has been done and is done, ideas might jump like grasshoppers in August.

One example of the kind of rut I'm talking about is the average church service. The church has used basically the same routine for at least 450 years.

We need to ask ourselves if this repetition is helpful or harmful. When did the church service last benefit from a new thought? How would you change the service? Are we incapable of altering it because it is perfect? Or are we so deeply inbred that all other ideas are dead from lack of oxygen?

Don't just muse over it. What are some ways you could improve it?

Ideas wait for no one. They must be chased, cornered, roped, and pulled to the ground. Ideas do not rush on us and force us to accept them. Christians are too often sitting and expecting a peculiar light. *Inspiration is reserved for those who pursue it.*

Creative people do not expect to be moved; *they* do the moving. Dreamers imagine themselves doing exciting things; creative people *do* them.

Do you want new ideas? Do you want to break out of the chains of dullness? Then organize a program which will produce creative ideas. Go after them; they seldom come after you.

Creativity is not an accident. The smart person will develop his own plan. Here is a suggestion for *planned creativity*. It is called the "I" plan. You could personalize it to your situation.

Information. Find out something about your idea. You don't have to be an expert, but you cannot be totally ignorant.

Use the local library. Question knowledgeable people. Collect basic information. Everyone can be for sea farming if they don't know anything about it. Don't confuse adverturous thinking with simple ignorance.

Isolation. Take the leisure time to get away and mull it over. Think without pressure.

Some business staffs are doing this with profit. Instead of working until the dim hours once a month, a few are planning weekend retreats. Twice a year they go to a resort and take their time. This allows them to brainstorm effectively.

You need your personal isolation time so ideas can incubate. Are you so busy performing that creative thinking is nearly impossible?

The isolation of a couple can also do wonders for their marriage.

Imagination. Let your mind go. Your mind

is one of the most magnificent resources in all of nature.

Your mind should be encouraged to make absurd suggestions. What seems ridiculous may be the exact idea you needed.

What would happen if you quit your job and started your own business? What would happen if you went back to school? What would happen if you disposed of your television set? Moved to Alaska? Started a summer project working with young people at a camp resort?

Investigation. Try your idea and see its effects. Dreaming is one thing, doing is another.

Your business and financial planning may be starving for your idea. Give it a trial run. The response may be sparkling.

If you get cold feet here, everything was useless. New ideas must find a place to get a start.

Integration. How does your idea fit into the total program? A mere shaving of an edge or a bending of a part may make the idea brilliant.

The temperament and thinking of your boss or family may determine any changes. The idea will not change, but you can improve the packaging to fit the expectation of the group.

A young man tried to publish a book about love, but publishers didn't want his manuscript. He changed the title to marriage and it was published immediately. It was the same idea exactly, but by making it fit into their genera concept he was able to move it.

Implementation. The bride walks to the front of the church, arm locked in her father's. Just before she takes the arm of the bridegroom she stops, removes her veil, and puts her flowers on a pew. "Thanks," she says, "I just wanted to see if I could do it." She pivots and leaves the church.

Often we fool with ideas. We want to see if we can do it, but we don't plan to complete the project.

What if we could calculate all the half-done ideas? How many were played with and then abandoned? Many of the ideas that you, I, and this society need may have been dumped in some trash heap. Because they were ditched it will take 5, 10, or 30 years for someone else to follow through with it.

Don't be a teaser of ideas. Never be content to merely tempt creativity. Only those who carry through are profitable contributors.

What role does God play in this process of creativity? He is the author of creation. God is the promoter of creativity. He is the enthusiast for creative thinking. He makes the process in your mind possible. God is pleased when you use your mind constructively.

"Whatever is good and perfect comes to us from God, the Creator of all light, and he shines forever without change or shadow" (James 1:17 TLB).

Several studies of creative people found them

to be sensitive. They had a caring, feeling personality as opposed to a cold and calculating one. They stop and think rather than merely produce.

Sensitivity must be prized in a technological age. Progress without caring is heartlessness.

Beware of the person who loses his bearing when he speaks of his business. If an employee is having health problems, would the boss let him go to increase company efficiency? Management argues, "But this is business," as if two distinct worlds exist. What is good for people is good for business, progress, and creativity. People are of more value than programs or sales charts. Efficiency cannot be allowed to smother people and devour creativity.

A truly creative company says that there are more important things than daily quotas. Because ideals and people count, they are willing to slow down and leave room to breathe.

What kind of creativity did it take a man to enter the Pike's Peak Marathon when he had no feet? Pete Strudwick was born with stumps but decided to enter the run. How does he begin to imagine he can do something as absurd as this?

As Pete passed runners on the route, what kind of thrill was it? His idea was more than a dream.

Where was God when Pete ran? We are sure of this: God was applauding an idea which refused to die.

Exercise

1. What idea have you had that you followed through with?
2. Where do you go to have a time to think and create?
3. Name one idea you would like to pursue. How will you start?
4. Do you have a physical handicap or mental restriction you would like to overcome? How can you start?

Chapter Thirteen

Your Mind Has A Steering Wheel

The human mind is like a bird in flight. It has to land someplace. The bird can choose a field of clover and lovely flowers. It can also decide to park in the city dump with its odors and refuse.

Your mind doesn't fly for long. Quickly it will light on a person, an automobile, a debt, an insult, a book, a television show, or the neighbor's property.

Too many of us believe that we have no control over where our mind settles. We act as if it rides the waves, helpless, without anchor or rudder.

The fact is that we each have strong, flexible minds. We bend, twist, and shape them fairly much any way we want. This is fantastic news to everyone who would like to lift up his mind and keep it on a higher, healthier plane.

In order to rise to new plateaus of creativity we must accept the responsibility for our own minds. If we perceive ourselves as victims we have limited creativity. We too easily blame our environment, our education, and our parents for the way we think. If this is the case we are helpless.

There is no doubt that many factors affect the way we think. However, we can drastically alter our frame of mind by merely assuming control. Often when we feel depressed we have allowed our minds to take the low road. When we pursue our dreams it is also because we have told our minds what to do.

Our pattern of thinking can change. That's the good news. We can take the steering wheels of our minds and assume control. When we do we will be pleased with the results.

We are not talking about a miracle. We are not suggesting that God will seize your brain and supernaturally realign your gray cells. The Bible says bluntly that you and I can control what we think.

Read this slowly: "Fix your thoughts on what is true and good and right. Think about things that are pure and lovely, and dwell on the fine, good things in others. Think about all you can praise God for and be glad about. Keep putting into practice all you learned from me and saw me doing, and the God of peace will be with you" (Philippians 4:8,9 TLB).

Picture your mind as having a large suction cup attached to it. With that suction cup I can tack my mind wherever I choose. Today I might stick my thoughts on someone who has treated me badly. All day my mind holds on like a sucking leech. Next I smack it on a personality trait of my own. I spend all day reminding myself how guilty I am. My day is miserable because I wasn't careful where I stuck my mind.

The Bible assures me that I can control where I stick it. Then it lists some of the best places to tack my thoughts. It only names eight good places. They are samples of all the others you could add.

All of us know someone like Larry. He was a nice guy, but for some reason all his thoughts seemed to run directly downhill. He had a tremendous need to find fault. You could tell him you had just climbed Mount McKinley, fought sharks in the Pacific, carried plasma to earthquake victims in Tibet, and rode wild horses through Siberia. After hearing all of that Larry would look at you and say, "Why don't you clean the dust off your glasses?"

Larry had to find something wrong. His personality, his security, his sense of values somehow demanded it.

That's why people didn't like to do things for Larry: They couldn't win. If you helped him move all day long, when the day was over he would mention the box you dropped. No thank you. No compliment. Larry had to prove that he could find fault.

Larry is a difficult friend to have. Most people don't stay around.

This personality trait is devastating in a parent. Imagine a child who cannot please his parents. The child can work himself into the ground, be careful to doublecheck everything, and still know that one thing is certain: When he is finished he will be criticized.

It's a no-win situation. It's caused by a person who refuses to control a mind that is crushingly negative.

There is good news for Larry and all his harmful cousins: Patterns of thinking can be changed! In most cases we can change the pattern ourselves. No lesser authority than the Bible says so.

Consequently there is hope for the non-creative, pedestrian thinker. If you have never done anything new and adventuresome, it is not too late. A mind that can head for the pits can also climb the heights. It is possible to saturate our minds with good thoughts, creative ideas, uplifting books, and great dreams.

There are certainly many evil aspects to life. We are surrounded by genuine hardships, injustices, and cruelty. However, if we attach our mind to these our pattern will become gloomy and hopeless. Our mind needs to visit these tragedies because they are harsh realities which do not go away. Yet visiting or even dealing with these cruelties is a far cry from living there. Even in the middle of ugliness our mind remains fixed someplace else. We cannot lose sight of beauty and hope, of goodness and purity.

A Christian policeman worked for several years on the vice squad. Eventually he had himself transferred. The continuous exposure to sordidness, deception, and degradation was taking a toll on his personality. Fortunately he could still see clearly enough to recognize what it was doing to him.

Most of us are too old to become baseball stars, skating beauties, or models. If we practiced for five years we might get better, but we aren't likely to land a contract with the Denver Broncos. Our body is limited, and in many ways those limitations will multiply with time.

However, our mind offers far greater potential for change than our body. It can maintain its flexibility and resilience for far more years.

I knew a man who was in his eighties. He had been through all the hard times. Drought and depression had rolled across his life, but he survived well. Illness had stricken his wife, but they still passed the fiftieth-anniversary mark.

Despite his years, hardship, and poor health, one characteristic burned bright: He was Mr. Encouragement. When much younger men were pessimistic, cautious, even distrusting, this man wanted to roll ahead. He wanted to dream, to go, to try.

It had nothing to do with age. His bright outlook was a reflection of his general disposition. If he could find a glimmer of hope, Mr. Encouragement was ready to chase it.

It was no accident that this man had Philippians 4:8 written on a plaque hanging on his wall.

There is no miracle involved; it doesn't take a secret formula hidden for centuries by Mongolian monks. The fact is that your mind has a steering wheel. Those who want a healthy, enjoyable outlook on life turn their minds in that direction. The more they turn that wheel the easier it becomes.

"If I should die before I wake" is part of a prayer that we remember from childhood. However, the fact is that many of us will die before we wake up to our real potential.

Inside most of us there is a stirring desire to try something. It might be a craft, a talent, a business, an adventure, possibly a career. Usually we put it off because of other pressing issues. We have children to raise, a home to establish, a garage to paint. The fact is that life will slide past without those dreams coming true. We will die before we wake to our real potential.

Almost ten years ago that reality hit me. In the back of my mind I have always wanted to write. During college and afterward I had published a few articles and frequently longed for a book.

Naturally there were other things to do—three children to raise and a career to chase. Then the harsh reality suddenly dawned: If I was not willing to write now, then when? I recognized the dream as a far-off oasis. It had no real form. It would never happen unless I made it happen.

One day I realized that it was time to make a decision. If my dream was to come true I had to reach out and grab it. There was no way it would come floating to me.

With a thousand dollars to our name we stepped out and never looked back. Years later we have completed 36 books and 100 magazine articles, and have traveled extensively to speak. Our dream came true. We did not die before we woke.

If we will not make our dream come true now, then when? We need a plan, a date, a definite form of action.

Exercise

Write two words on a piece of paper: up▲ and down▼. Keep a record of how many uplifting thoughts you have today and how many downers. You can do it by simple marks. Keep a similar record tomorrow. Watch the "up" column increase and the "down" column decrease because you want it to.

Chapter Fourteen

The Power Of Negative Thinking

The person who agrees with everything may have a mummified mind. Too much contentment is a bad thing. A totally contented person cannot progress. He sees everything as fine. He rocks himself to sleep.

Many needed advances are left begging merely because most of us are sadly tranquil. Creative negativism says that there are some things that could be better and I'm going to change them.

Let's divide negative thinking into three types. They overlap, but each gives us a handle to work with.

First is the *iconoclast*. He wants to tear

141

everything down if it is established and older than three months. He says, "Get rid of the past!"

This person isn't all wrong. He will remove some old evils. The problem is his shotgun approach. Because he is so negative, many good things will also be toppled.

Second is the *professional cynic*. He complains and complains but does nothing. This sourlip knows what is wrong with everything, but he takes no action. There is no effort to remove or improve. His total effect is a sigh or gripe. The cynic does no one any good.

The third type is the *creative negativist*. This person sees things that are wrong, has hope, and does something about them. He taps the power of negative thinking.

Often negativism is a sign of intelligence. But the first two groups are restricted and often dangerous. The third group is the one which will remodel and hopefully regenerate the world.

Thousands of people are frankly bored. They are surrounded by stale, routine, unimaginative monotony.

If you are bored, great! There is hope! Go ahead and admit it. Sometimes you want to scream. That's fantastic. Say aloud, "There is something wrong." Louder. "THERE IS SOMETHING WRONG!"

You have bounced up on the *first* step of creative negative thinking. It is a small step, but you aren't where you used to be. You have admitted there is a problem.

Now leap to the *second* step: You would like to do something about it. Beautiful. You have the will to change and improve. Don't stop now.

Jump to the *third* step. What would help the situation? What kind of surgery, injection, or therapy will it need? Don't settle for a Band-Aid. If you do, you could soon lapse back into the same sleeping sickness.

After you have hashed out a solution, hop up on the *fourth* step: Put it to work. The first three plateaus are useless if you are afraid of the fourth. You are still too low to see over the hump. Come on, do it! Take that fourth jump. You may not get this high again.

On the fourth step you joined such daring notables as Jesus Christ Himself. He looked at His situation and screamed, "There is something wrong!" The synagogues and temple were bigoted against certain races. The laws of the Pharisees were ugly concrete blocks. Widows were being ripped off by the religious leaders. Sinners were being hated instead of loved.

Jesus said it was wrong. Not only did He object, but on that fourth step He offered the people something better. Christ gave them Himself.

Good negative thinking is hard to find partly because we have become familiar with sameness. Suppose your club begins every meeting by each member blowing his nose. That sounds dumb. But do it for a while and after months or years it will seem like the normal way to start a meeting.

We are surrounded by absurdities. We have

done them so long that they no longer seem ridiculous. We need a wiggly worm to pop his head out of the group and say "Wrong!"

Can you imagine the negative thinking of the philosopher John Locke? Before the American Revolution two premises were accepted as eternal truth: Most people believed in the divine right of kings, and also in a form of caste system. If you were born a lumberjack you were meant to be one. You worked 12-14 hours a day and never expected to change.

Locke wiggled to the top and said that both were wrong. He said that people who didn't want a king did not have to keep one. Locke also said that every man had a right to individual happiness. It was not reserved for the nobleman.

Easy ideas? They weren't then. Locke had to go into exile for resisting the accepted. However, those who are Locke fans claim that he is the father of the French, English, and American Revolutions.

Most of us are being pampered because we go along with the status quo. We are like trained seals: If we blow the horn at the correct time we get a chunk of fish. The seal has learned to enjoy this and wouldn't consider disagreeing.

Carry this principle into marriage. There are thousands of divorces every year because both partners are bored. There is no specific serious problem, but not knowing what else to do they call it quits.

The couple came to the place of negative thinking. They agreed that their marriage was dull.

They took step one. Too bad they couldn't step up to the power of negative thinking and want, find, and put into action the proper solution. They could have made plans to add creative life and hope.

A person resigns his job simply because it's boring. In many cases he is the victim of his own lack of imagination. There may be ways to bring zest to his occupation. He got on the first step of discontent but could not make his way up to the fourth.

Eric Sevareid of CBS claimed that the basic cause for World War I may have been boredom. People who had nothing exciting to do were unable to channel their negative feelings constructively.

Many housewives complain of the same ailment. Some are finding good outlets as mothers at home. Millions are going into the labor market. Those who can find no creative alternatives are often turning to alcohol. Still others are suffering from acute mental illness.

Are you fed up? Disgusted? Bored? A little angry? Find a creative solution to negative thinking.

This is where a faith in the living God goes to work. If you believe that God has productive solutions you ask Him to remold your thinking.

Part of what holds us back is our victim complex. We often feel we are helpless on the raging seas of life, tossed here and there and unable to change our course or circumstances.

Nonsense. As long as we feel like victims

we will sink in self-pity.

No one is saying that you can do everything. That's foolish dreaming. But you can do *far more* than what you are doing.

James Michener did not write his first book until he was 40 years old. That book, *South Pacific,* launched him into an amazing career lasting over 30 years.

In the process of putting negative power to work, watch out for the experienced sourpuss. He is the person who tells you he has tried everything and he knows nothing will work. He is Mr. No. Watch out! He turns dreams into nightmares.

If you ask him if it can be done cheaper, his reply is no, he has tried it. If you ask him if tomatoes will grow on this ground he says, "No, I tried it in '29." Can you open a new business in town? No way—that part of town is dying. His attitude will rub off if you keep listening to him.

If at all possible, try to associate with people who dream. They see problems and imagine solutions. Attitudes are contagious. Though we want to be independent thinkers, our surroundings do affect our disposition.

You don't want to wait any longer. That important change has waited long enough. Start now to plot a solution to the problem you know must be met.

Exercise

1. Think of a real problem you face. List three things you could do to creatively change that situation.
2. Name something you do which is genuinely boring. What one thing could you do to give it life?
3. How do you rate yourself?
   a. Negative—tear everything down
   b. Cynic—criticize and do nothing
   c. Creative negativist
   d. Content—make no changes
4. Do you see yourself as getting things done or do you see yourself as a helpless victim of circumstances? Explain.
5. When was the last time you took charge and changed something? Explain.

Chapter Fifteen

Experimenting

Are you ready to try? Is your creative saliva percolating? There is a pulsating world all around us waiting for the small or large thing you have to contribute.

Ask John Snyder what it's like. He is a chemical engineer who loves studying maps. John didn't love cartography enough to get formal training. He just piddled with it.

In the process of tinkering he found that experts couldn't figure out how to make accurate maps from satellites. For a year Snyder accepted it as a challenge. Every weekend he pushed equations around.

In 1978 the U.S. Geological Survey presented Snyder with a special award. They were indebted to what the engineer had devised even though the most serious professionals in the field weren't able to pull it off.

Are your creative juices moving? The whole world is God's creative oyster. Why not be part of it?

How did John Gorrie invent the ice-making machine? What about John Walker's friction match? Or Percy Spencer's microwave oven? How would you like to have been Edwin Land and have invented the Polaroid camera?

What were the secrets to these creative wonders? One thing is certain: They were willing to experiment and try.

Were these men geniuses? In many cases they had ordinary to dismal beginnings.

Einstein essentially flunked youth. He was considered retarded. He did so poorly in languages that his teacher asked him to drop the class. Einstein barely got into college and graduated by a miracle. The great mind couldn't get a job teaching, and only by pulling strings did he get a job at the patent office.

Is this the material from which the greatest genius of our time was cut? Then there is tremendous hope for *me;* I flunked more things than he did!

He could have folded up in self-pity. The next 50 years could have been spent feeling sorry for himself. Instead he tried what he enjoyed and opened like a tulip.

Before you begin to experiment, learn to distinguish two types of thinking: One is deductive, the other inductive. They aren't difficult concepts. You will learn them quickly.

Deductive reasoning says the world is round. Then follows evidence to prove it is round. Inductive reasoning says I am not sure what shape the earth may be. Let's start gathering evidence.

Deductive thinking starts off with a premise and tries to prove it. Inductive is wide open, willing to go wherever the facts lead.

Most of the time we think deductively while insisting it is inductive.

Deductive thinking is locked in. It knows the answer before it begins. Inductive thinking is an adventure. It is a far more open posture.

Deductive thinking is comfortable. Less questioning and research needs to go on. It is also less productive.

An inductive attitude says, "Beats me what will happen. Let's find out."

If you drop a bowling ball it will fall to the floor. Good deductive reasoning. If you drop the same ball and are waiting to see where it will go, you are thinking inductively.

Try an inductive approach in your home. Ask your children to help you solve your television-viewing problem. Their decision will not be binding, but you would like to hear their solution. How would they guarantee a good balance of time spent watching TV? Which shows would they approve and disapprove? Would they leave

TV-watching entirely up to each individual?

Don't assume you know what they will say. Give them a chance. You may find practical and fair suggestions.

There is risk in this. Their opinions may be the exact opposite of yours. Their suggestions may be absurd. That is the risk of creative experimentation. Don't be afraid to be open-ended.

We tried a similar experiment at our home. We allowed the children to watch anything they wanted. The only catch was that they had to critique the shows. Their ages were 12, 10, and 8. We gave them a sheet of paper for each problem. The paper had items to grade: sex, language, violence, fun, good purpose, helpful hero, etc.

This was a learning experiment for all of us. In some cases they were forced to admit certain objectionable facts. In other instances we had to confess we were wrong.

Where are the lumps in your family pudding? Some of them could be smoothed out by inductive experimentation.

This is exactly the problem Jesus faced as He attempted to minister to people. They said in essence, "Go away, we already know what God is like. You do not match our deductive pattern." Closed minds turned Him off.

Those who think they have all the answers are missing too much by blind dogmatism. In the process of experimenting you will open wide the gates for the people you affect. You will inject them with a creative spirit of adventure.

Perhaps you are wondering if children can be allowed the luxury of experimenting, since they don't have experience. Remember, sometimes experience is the enemy of experimental thinking rather than its friend.

An ant has a brain the size of a pinhead. Its experience is restricted, but ants are expertly capable of solving problems. Ants can calculate a situation and adapt to its changes. An ant can remember where it has been. Dr. Stephen Bernstein has noted that simple wood ants actually solve problems (*Science Digest,* Feb. 1979).

Too often we sell our complicated minds short. People of all ages are better problem-solvers than we may realize.

If you want to experiment with interesting but harmless fun, try this with your family tonight. Design a better chair. There are no restrictions and you can use whatever material you want to. After the initial explanation, offer only support as each draws a chair. "That's a great idea." "Yes, it can hang from the ceiling." "Yes, we can get 100 orange juice cans if you need them."

The next time design a lamp. How about a family cottage if money were no object? How would you design a better baseball glove?

Try an experiment in creative writing. Ask each person to write one paragraph describing how their life might change if their cat had chicks.

Are you looking for something more serious? You will be living in a dormitory for three weeks. Your job is to convince the students that Jesus is the Son of God. How would you go about it?

In order to be good at experimenting, an individual has to see failure as a friend. If you are uptight, if winning is all important, you make a poor creative experimenter.

Something does not have to succeed for it to be valuable. There is also merit in discovering that a method or plan is not plausible. The person who tries is the true success. The only failures are the ones who never leave the gate.

Irving Langmuir was one of the special breed who learned to appreciate failure. It took him six years to discover the correct balance for the tungsten filament. Because he built failure upon failure he was finally able to climb high enough to revolutionize the light bulb.

Failures are successes if they do not stop us. Each failure in creative experiments is one less thing you need to try. Consequently, you are one step closer to victory.

When you enter an experiment you learn something no matter how it turns out. Maybe the announcement has to eventually come, "It was a good try but it didn't work." And maybe you will announce just the opposite.

The Bible is packed with experiments. Some of them worked out and others were disasters. Barnabas decided to give Paul a chance and introduce him to the disciples. Could the old Christian-killer have backfired? You know it.

Often success is a bucket of cold water to creative experiments. An individual is successful at manufacturing nuts and bolts. He has accumulated a large amount of money and all the accompanying creature comforts.

Why should he take a chance by trying to produce lint brushes? If he expands into this area, he takes the chance of losing thousands of dollars. If it flops, he will look like an idiot.

He sits back to rest on his dignified past. The spirit of adventure has broken down into contentment. He is like the retired Indian scout resigned to telling tall tales of his amazing career.

Has your spirit of experiment died the death of success? Why take unnecessary chances? You have stagnated under your own accomplishment.

The creative person does not drive looking out his rearview mirror. He moves looking ahead. He finds tomorrow exciting.

Make the world your laboratory. Your home is filled with biological, geometric, and behavioral science test tubes. Your classroom is the thrilling test grounds for the educational science of tomorrow. You may teach a Sunday school class which is a spiritual greenhouse where Christians can be planted, watered, and nurtured.

Truth is an unfolding rose. When we first see the flower, we have seen a rose. Under close investigation the petals open. With each petal we see more of the rose, and yet it always remains a rose.

Christian thought has nothing to fear from creative experimenting. All truth is of benefit. Only ignorance or lies are enemies.

When was the last time you changed your socks? When was the last time you tried a significant change in your lifestyle, entertainment, school, or job? Fortunately the answer to both questions tells us different things about ourselves.

A college history professor was telling me about a teaching tool he used in class. He has the class reenact a famous courtroom scene. At a dramatic moment he introduced evidence which supposedly would clear the defendant.

I asked him what would happen if his student jury did not agree with the former verdict. The professor explained coolly that he was willing to take the results any way they came. Experimenting came easy to him.

Take these same risks. Give a problem to your class to solve however they will. Was Judas's sadness really an act of repentance or not? Was Caiaphas historically correct in being afraid of Jesus Christ? Would John the Baptist's dress and methods be effective in our society? If you find these experiments successful, you might want to tackle capital punishment. If you do, let the jury rule and you keep quiet.

Experimental teaching is not for the dogmatic.

Neither is it for the sheepish. Once you launch the vessel you must let it find its own port.

The entire world of experimenting is a mind-stretching, exciting life. Its key word is *try.*

Exercise

1. Prepare a television "test" for your family or class. Discuss your results.
2. Name one object (mousetrap, door handle, screwdriver, lawn mower, etc.) that you would like to see improved. How?
3. Draw a shirt or blouse. Use your own design. Be original.
4. Design a book. Have it look and open differently from what we are used to.